Trees of Central Florida

TREES
of Central Florida

By Olga Lakela and
Richard P. Wunderlin

With the Collaboration
of Pierre Genelle
and Glenn Fleming

BANYAN BOOKS
Miami, Florida

Copyright © 1980 by
Olga Lakela and Richard P. Wunderlin

No part of this book may be reproduced
or utilized in any form without permission
in writing from the publisher except by a reviewer
who wishes to quote brief passages
for the purpose of a review.

Designed by Bernard Lipsky

Manufactured in the United States of America

Illustration credits:
All photographs by Pierre Genelle and Glenn Fleming

Library of Congress Cataloging in Publication Data

Lakela, Olga.
   Trees of central Florida.
   Includes index.
   1. Trees—Florida—Identification.   I. Title.
QK484.F6L34   582.1609759   80-12797
ISBN 0-916224-51-1

Contents

List of Illustrations   *6*
Preface   *9*
Introduction   *11*
Key to Identification of Families   *17*
Descriptive Flora   *23*
Glossary   *198*
Index to Scientific and Common Names   *205*

Illustrations

1. Map of Florida counties and range of manual *12*
2. *Pinus clausa* (Sand Pine) *24*
3. *Taxodium ascendens* (Pond Cypress) *26*
4. *Chamaecyparis thyoides* (Atlantic White Cedar) *29*
5. *Juniperus silicicola* (Southern Red Cedar) *30*
6. *Sabal palmetto* (Cabbage Palm) *31*
7. *Washingtonia robusta* (Desert Palm) *33*
8. *Casuarina litorea* (Australian Pine) *34*
9. *Salix caroliniana* (Carolina Willow) *36*
10. *Myrica cerifera* (Wax Myrtle) *37*
11. *Carya aquatica* (Water Hickory) *39*
12. *Carpinus caroliniana* (American Hornbeam) *41*
13. *Ostrya virginiana* (Hop Hornbeam) *43*
14. *Quercus nigra* (Water Oak) *46*
15. *Celtis laevigata* (Hackberry) *49*
16. *Trema micranthum* (Nettle Tree) *50*
17. *Ulmus americana* (American Elm) *52*
18. *Broussonetia papyrifera* (Paper Mulberry) *54*
19. *Ficus aurea* (Strangler Fig) *55*
20. *Maclura pomifera* (Osage Orange) *57*
21. *Morus alba* (White Mulberry) *58*
22. *Schoepfia chrysophylloides* (Graytwig) *59*
23. *Ximenia americana* (Tallowwood) *60*
24. *Coccoloba uvifera* (Sea Grape) *62*
25. *Gaupira discolor* (Blolly) *64*
26. *Liriodendron tulipifera* (Tulip Tree) *65*
27. *Magnolia virginiana* (Sweet Bay) *67*
28. *Illicium parviflorum* (Star Anise) *68*
29. *Annona glabra* (Pond Apple) *70*
30. *Asimina parviflora* (Dwarf Pawpaw) *71*
31. *Cinnamomum camphora* (Camphor Tree) *72*
32. *Nectandra coriacea* (Lancewood) *74*
33. *Persea borbonia* (Redbay) *76*
34. *Sassafras albidum* (Sassafras) *77*

35. *Capparis flexuosa* (Limber Caper) *79*
36. *Hamamelis virginiana* (Witch-hazel) *80*
37. *Liquidambar styraciflua* (Sweet Gum) *81*
38. *Crataegus marshallii* (Parsley Haw) *84*
39. *Prunus caroliniana* (Carolina Laurel Cherry) *86*
40. *Chrysobalanus icaco* (Cocoplum) *87*
41. *Acacia farnesiana* (Sweet Acacia) *90*
42. *Albizia lebbeck* (Woman's Tongue) *91*
43. *Bauhinia variegata* (Orchid Tree) *93*
44. *Cassia coluteoides* (Cassia) *94*
45. *Cercis canadensis* (Redbud) *95*
46. *Delonix regia* (Royal Poinciana) *96*
47. *Enterolobium cyclocarpa* (Earpod Tree) *98*
48. *Gleditsia aquatica* (Water Locust) *99*
49. *Leucaena leucocephala* (Jumbie-bean) *100*
50. *Parkinsonia aculeata* (Jerusalem Thorn) *102*
51. *Piscidia piscipula* (Jamaica Dogwood) *103*
52. *Pithecellobium unguis-cati* (Cat's Claw) *105*
53. *Tamarindus indica* (Tamarind) *106*
54. *Amyris elemifera* (Torchwood) *107*
55. *Citrus aurantium* (Sour Orange) *109*
56. *Ptelea trifoliata* (Hop Tree) *110*
57. *Zanthoxylum clava-herculis* (Hercules' Club) *112*
58. *Simarouba glauca* (Paradise Tree) *114*
59. *Suriana maritima* (Bay Cedar) *115*
60. *Bursera simaruba* (Gumbo Limbo) *117*
61. *Melia azedarach* (Chinaberry) *118*
62. *Swietenia mahagoni* (Mahogany) *119*
63. *Drypetes lateriflora* (Guiana Plum) *121*
64. *Sapium sebiferum* (Popcorn Tree) *122*
65. *Mangifera indica* (Mango) *124*
66. *Metopium toxiferum* (Poisonwood) *125*
67. *Rhus copallina* (Winged Sumac) *127*
68. *Schinus terebinthifolius* (Brazilian Pepper Tree) *128*
69. *Cyrilla racemiflora* (Titi) *129*
70. *Ilex cassine* (Dahoon) *131*
71. *Maytenus phyllanthoides* (Gutta-percha) *133*
72. *Acer rubrum* (Southern Red Maple) *135*
73. *Aesculus pavia* (Red Buckeye) *137*
74. *Exothea paniculata* (Inkwood) *138*
75. *Sapindus marginatus* (Florida Soapberry) *140*
76. *Krugiodendron ferreum* (Black Ironwood) *141*
77. *Rhamnus caroliniana* (Carolina Buckthorn) *143*
78. *Muntingia calabura* (Strawberry Tree) *144*
79. *Tilia caroliniana* (Carolina Basswood) *146*

80. *Hibiscus tiliaceus* (Mahoe)   *147*
81. *Gordonia lasianthus* (Loblolly Bay)   *148*
82. *Carica papaya* (Papaya)   *150*
83. *Rhizophora mangle* (Red Mangrove)   *151*
84. *Conocarpus erecta* (Buttonwood)   *153*
85. *Laguncularia racemosa* (White Mangrove)   *154*
86. *Eugenia axillaris* (White Stopper)   *156*
87. *Melaleuca quinquenervia* (Cajeput)   *158*
88. *Myrcianthes fragrans* (Twinberry)   *159*
89. *Psidium guajava* (Guava)   *161*
90. *Nyssa sylvatica* (Black Gum)   *162*
91. *Aralia spinosa* (Devil's Walkingstick)   *164*
92. *Cornus florida* (Flowering Dogwood)   *165*
93. *Lyonia ferruginea* (Rusty Lyonia)   *166*
94. *Vaccinium arboreum* (Sparkleberry)   *167*
95. *Jacquinia keyensis* (Joewood)   *169*
96. *Ardisia escallonioides* (Marlberry)   *170*
97. *Rapanea punctata*   *172*
98. *Bumelia celastrina* (Saffron Plum)   *174*
99. *Chrysophyllum oliviforme* (Satinleaf)   *175*
100. *Manilkara zapota* (Sapodilla)   *176*
101. *Mastichodendron foetidissimum* (Wild Mastic)   *178*
102. *Diospyros virginiana* (Persimmon)   *179*
103. *Symplocos tinctoria* (Sweetleaf)   *180*
104. *Chionanthus virginicus* (Fringe Tree)   *182*
105. *Forestiera segregata* (Florida Privet)   *183*
106. *Fraxinus caroliniana* (Pop Ash)   *185*
107. *Osmanthus americana* (Devilwood)   *186*
108. *Cordia sebestena* (Geiger Tree)   *187*
109. *Citharexylum fruticosum* (Fiddlewood)   *189*
110. *Avicennia germinans* (Black Mangrove)   *190*
111. *Casasia clusiifolia* (Seven-year Apple)   *192*
112. *Cephalanthus occidentalis* (Buttonbush)   *193*
113. *Pinckneya bracteata* (Fever Tree)   *194*
114. *Viburnum obovatum* (Black Haw)   *196*
115. *Baccharis halimifolia* (Groundsel Tree)   *197*

Preface

Florida has long been noted for its great diversity of tree life. Over 300 species can be found in the state, which are about half of all known trees in North America, north of Mexico. It is, therefore, not surprising to learn that there are more different kinds of trees in Florida than in any other state in the Union.

This manual is offered for the use of all who are interested in knowing how to identify the common native trees of central Florida. This area is defined as extending from Levy, Marion, and Volusia counties south to Lee, Hendry, and Broward counties. In this area, we have one of the richest tree floras in the state. Traveling from north to south one can see a transition from predominantly warm temperate to tropical vegetation in a relatively short span of miles.

This guide was prepared so that anyone with an interest in knowing trees would be able to do so. Photographs are used throughout to facilitate identification of species. We are much indebted to Mr. Glenn Fleming and Mr. Pierre Genelle for their photography, which has made the illustrations possible, and for their assistance with the text. We also wish to thank the staff of the University Herbarium and of the Department of Biology, University of South Florida for their assistance during the preparation of this work. Special acknowledgment is due the late Dr. Robert W. Long, under whose guidance the initial draft of this work was produced.

O.L.
R.P.W.

Tampa, Florida
January, 1980

Introduction

The purpose of this book is to enable a person to identify the common native trees of subtropical Florida. This area covers 30 counties extending from Levy, Marion, and Volusia counties in the north through Lee, Hendry, and Broward counties in the south (Fig. 1). This area is floristically very rich with both tropical and temperate species. The trees found to the north tend to be predominately temperate species related to the flora that extends southward from the Appalachians, whereas many of the trees in the southern part of the area have tropical affinities. In certain places tropical species may be found growing far up the coast where they are sufficiently protected from severe frost.

How to Use the Keys

Although we have attempted to make the process of identification as understandable as possible by means of photographs of actual tree specimens (a representative species of each genus is illustrated), the surest way of determining the name of the plant is by tracing it step by step through the keys. Usually using the keys is also the quickest way to positive identification even though you may be tempted to take a short cut by referring to the photographs.

The keys in the front of this book are based as much as possible on the vegetative characters of the tree, particularly those of the leaf and stem. We have endeavored to avoid the use of technical language, but certain terms must be used and some of these may be unfamiliar. The glossary at the end of the book will be most helpful for those of you who have little experience with plant keys. Familiarity with the basic terminology enables you to quickly learn how to use the identification keys. To ensure the greatest ease in the use of these keys, they are based on the method of two contrasting alternatives: for example, 1) leaves simple *or* 1) leaves compound. The two alternatives are indicated by having the same number. Having made your choice, you will find either

12 Trees of Central Florida

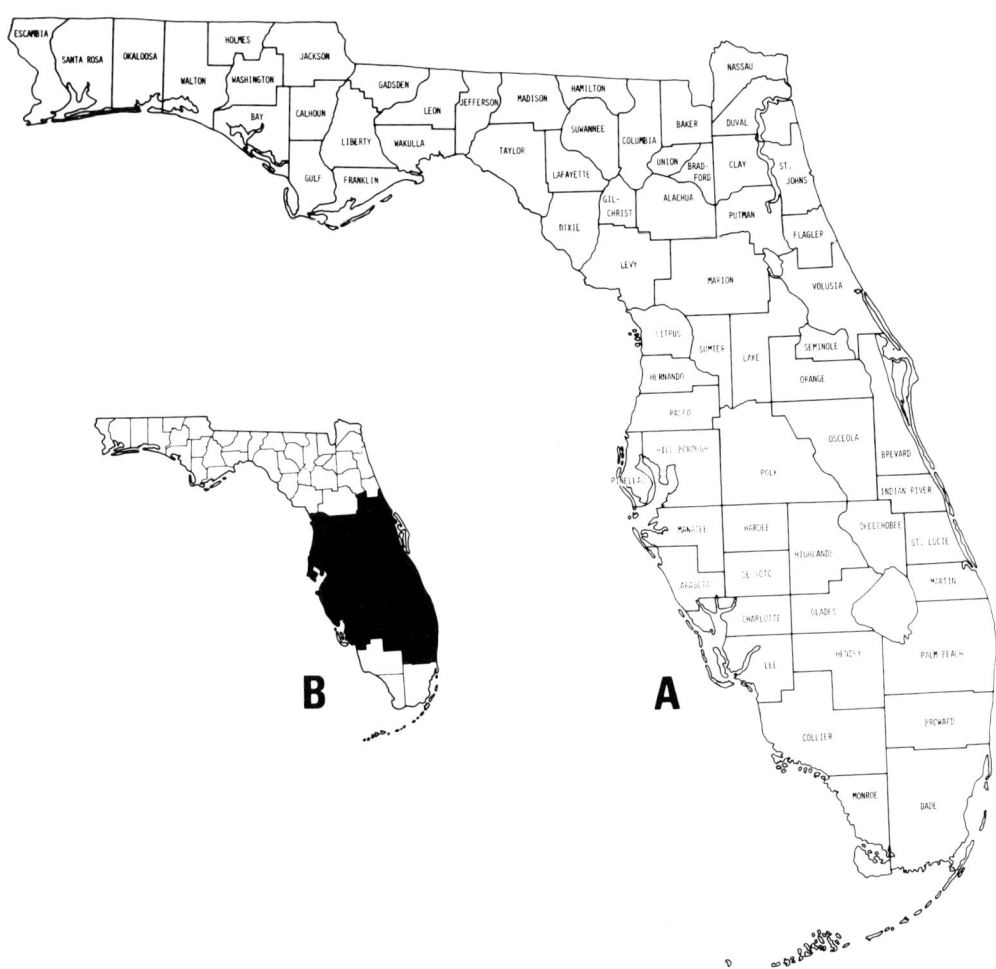

Fig. 1. Map of Florida counties (A) and range of manual (B).

a number or scientific species, genus, or family name at the end of the statement. If a number is given, go to the pair of alternatives indicated by that number. Continue on in this fashion until your choice leads to a species name. At every step you should consider both alternatives before making a choice because one may help explain the other. For successfully using the key, you must make accurate observations of the structure in question, and you must know the meaning of the descriptive words that are used in the keys. In general, identification will be greatly facilitated by using a simple hand lens with approximately a 10-power magnification. A number of types of hand lenses are presently on the market and will be a worthwhile purchase.

Verification of Specimens

After a given specimen has been traced through the keys, occasionally you still may be unsure about the correct name for the plant. Even experienced naturalists will occasionally collect a very unusual or puzzling form. In such cases comparisons with authentic material must be made in a good herbarium or a professional botanist must be consulted. In the area specifically covered by this book the University of South Florida Herbarium serves as a repository of plant specimens; the staff will be pleased to provide the service of confirming plant identifications. Fresh specimens may be sent through the mail if they are placed in plastic bags or wrap, in wax paper, or in a small box. Sometimes it may become necessary to send dried specimens. In this instance, the plants should be pressed between pieces of cardboard and securely wrapped. Plant specimens can be sent by ordinary parcel post. For accurate determinations both flowers and fruits are desirable and occasionally absolutely necessary. This fact should be remembered when collecting specimens.

Names of Plants

This book includes the common names and Latin or scientific names for the plants. They are listed according to the family to which they belong, and the families follow the standard enumeration presently used in floras. The authors of species names are given immediately following the epithet. Characteristic habitat or ecological information is given for each species as an aid in identifying the plant. This information is based upon records in the university herbarium. The principal plant associations in the Central Florida area are wet and dry pine flatwoods, sandhills, coastal dunes and strand, freshwater swamps, mangrove shores, hammocks, and oak–pine scrub vegetation. If more specific habitat descriptions are available, they are also included with the species notes. Synonyms or names by which the species has been called in other books are given in some cases if such use is frequent. Limitations of space have prevented us from giving all the synonyms, but some are included for reference. An index to the scientific and common names is provided at the end of the book.

Vegetational Formations

Peninsular Florida is the emergent part of a much larger section of continental North America that was separated from the continent by a seaway during geological times. Much of Florida was an island, but later it was united to the mainland. Repeated submergences have resulted in inland marine deposits throughout the area.

The soils of this region support seven major vegetation formations that can be identified for the range of this manual. 1) *Pine Flatwoods* – This is the most extensive plant formation in the area. These are open woods dominated by the longleaf pine, slash pine, and saw palmetto. Hardwood hammocks, cypress swamps, marshes, and prairies are often scattered throughout this formation. 2) *Xerophytic Pine–Oak Forests* – In the northern half of this manual range, the forests are characterized by slash pine and xerophytic scrub oak associations that occur mostly on well-drained uplands. Many of these regions have now been cleared for citrus groves. 3) *Mangrove Associations and Coastal Marshes* – The three mangrove species – red mangrove, black mangrove, white mangrove – and buttonwood are found in tidal areas that vary from saline to brackish. These plants are tropical species, but nevertheless they often form dense vegetation in habitats along the coasts, and they are especially well developed along the many inlets and bays. 4) *Coastal Strand* – This is a tropical association found along the coastal shores. Although it does not include important tree species, it does have a number of important pioneer herbs and shrubs of wide distribution. The plants are characteristic of the dune formations and sandy soils above the high-tide mark. 5) *Swamp Forests* – Two important associations are found in the low, flooded ground. The first is the cypress swamp with bald cypress and various hardwood species, such as red maple and water ash. The second is the hardwood swamp characterized by black gum, loblolly bay, red bay, and sweet bay. These forests are often highly mixed formations bordering rivers and basins. They often form thick masses of vegetation that are then called hammocks. 6) *Sand-Pine Scrub Forests* — This formation is well developed in central Florida with relatively small areas occurring elsewhere. The characteristic species are sand pine and rosemary. This formation occurs on well-drained, deep, white, sandy soils and especially on old dunes in interior regions. 7) *Grasslands* — These are either wet prairies on seasonally flooded lowlands or dry prairies on less frequently flooded flatlands found particularly in the southern and central portion of the manual range. Many of the areas formerly occupied by grasslands are now improved pastureland.

Many of us would like to know what the plant formations looked like 100 or even 500 years ago. The great changes in Florida have made it difficult to imagine what the virgin land must have been like. Dredge-and-fill operations have greatly altered the landscape, eliminating many of the former habitats. Probably as a result, fewer native species are in this area than were formerly. Unfortunately, now we have no way of knowing the extent of change in the composition of our forests. On the other hand, due to the activities and interests of man, new or exotic trees have been introduced and naturalized within our area. Two introduced trees that are now common are the Australian pine and Brazilian pepper. Another example of an introduced weed tree species is the cajeput tree. These and other introduced plants compete with, and in many cases crowd out, the native trees. Sometimes tree species in our area are neither naturalized nor native; but, rather, they are cultivated plants that are unable to reproduce outside of cultivation. These species are not included in this book.

We have included the general range of distribution for species as they exist in our range and also as they extend outside of Florida. In general, the distribution is given for Florida, then to the west and to the north. Distribution information is often important in placing a given tree species in perspective regarding the habitat of the species.

The woody vegetation of central Florida is to many people the most interesting element of the flora. These plants give our region its characteristic appearance. The palms, conifers, and hardwood species are the plants that most people think of when they think of Florida. This manual makes it possible for Florida residents and visitors to become familiar with the great diversity of our tree life.

Key to Identification of Families

1. Leaves needlelike, scalelike, or linear 2
1. Leaves with broad blades 5
   2. Branches cylindrical, jointed, needlelike; leaves scalelike, in whorls of 6 or more at joints ...... CASUARINACEAE (p. 32)
   2. Branches cylindrical or angled, not jointed; leaves linear, scalelike or needlelike (if scalelike, then not more than 3 at a node) 3
3. Leaves needlelike, in fascicles .... PINACEAE (p. 23)
3. Leaves scalelike or linear 4
   4. Leaves evergreen, scalelike .... CUPRESSACEAE (p. 27)
   4. Leaves deciduous, linear .... TAXODIACEAE (p. 25)
5. Leaves with parallel veins; trunk unbranched ... ARECACEAE (p. 28)
5. Leaves with netlike veins; trunk branched 6
   6. Leaves opposite (or mostly so) or whorled 7
   6. Leaves all alternate 24
7. Leaves compound 8
7. Leaves simple 10
   8. Leaves pinnately compound or 3-foliolate 9
   8. Leaves palmately compound ... HIPPOCASTANACEAE (p. 136)
9. Leaf scars *V*-shaped; fruit a united pair of samaras .... ACERACEAE (p. 132)
9. Leaf scars shield-shaped; fruit a single samara .. OLEACEAE (p. 181)
   10. Leaves palmately nerved .... ACERACEAE (p. 132)
   10. Leaves pinnately nerved 11
11. Leaves evergreen 12
11. Leaves deciduous 21
    12. Leaves glandular-punctuate below ...... MYRTACEAE (p. 152)
    12. Leaves not glandular-punctuate below 13
13. Trees with conspicuous aerial proroots .... RHIZOPHORACEAE (p. 149)
13. Trees without conspicuous aerial proroots 14
    14. Petioles with a pair of apical glands . COMBRETACEAE (p. 152)
    14. Petioles without a pair of apical glands 15
15. Stipular scars encircling stem 16

15. Stipular scars not encircling stem 18
    16. Leaves whitish-pubescent below ...AVICENNIACEAE (p. 188)
    16. Leaves glabrate below 17
17. Flowers or fruits in pendent racemes; fruit single-seeded,
    less than 1 cm long .... VERBENACEAE (p. 187)
17. Flowers or fruits in terminal or axillary cymes;
    fruit many-seeded, 5-8 cm long .... RUBIACEAE (p. 188)
    18. Twigs with dense pubescence; leaf margin
        undulate .... RHAMNACEAE (p. 139)
    18. Twigs other than with dense pubescence; leaf margin
        not undulate 19
19. Leaves less than 5 cm long 20
19. Leaves over 5 cm long .... OLEACEAE (p. 181)
    20. Fruit an orange berry .... THEOPHRASTACEAE (p. 168)
    20. Fruit a light-brown, cylindrical nutlet enclosed in a red,
        fleshy calyx-tube .... NYCTAGINACEAE (p. 61)
21. Stipular scars encircling the stem 22
21. Stipular scars not encircling the stem .... OLEACEAE (p. 181)
    22. Tertiary veins of leaves all parallel; flowers subtended
        by 4 large petaloid bracts .... CORNACEAE (p. 163)
    22. Leaves and flowers not as above 23
23. Flowers subtended by a single petaloid bract or in a dense
    globose head .... RUBIACEAE (p. 188)
23. Flowers not subtended by a single petaloid bract nor in a
    dense globose head .... CAPRIFOLIACEAE (p. 191)
    24. Leaves compound 25
    24. Leaves simple 37
25. Leaves toothed (sometimes minutely so) 26
25. Leaves entire or merely undulate 31
    26. Leaves twice-compound 27
    26. Leaves once-compound 28
27. Stem spiny .... ARALIACEAE (p. 160)
27. Stem not spiny .... MELIACEAE (p. 117)
    28. Flowers in catkins .... JUGLANDACEAE (p. 38)
    28. Flowers not in catkins 29
29. Leaflets 1 to 3 .... RUTACEAE (p. 104)
29. Leaflets 5 or more 30
    30. Fruit a 1- to 3-seeded, flattened legume ..... FABACEAE (p. 88)
    30. Fruit a drupe .... ANACARDIACEAE (p. 123)
31. Ovaries 3 to many, distinct or nearly so ..SIMAROUBACEAE (p. 111)
31. Ovary 1, simple or compound 32
    32. Leaves even-pinnate 33
    32. Leaves odd-pinnate 34
33. Fruit a legume .... FABACEAE (p. 88)
33. Fruit a berry .... SAPINDACEAE (p. 136)

Key to Identification of Families   19

    34. Flowers in terminal racemes, panicles, or cymes 35
    34. Flowers in lateral or axillary clusters 36
35. Flowers in cymes or panicles .... ANACARDIACEAE (p. 123)
35. Flowers in racemes .... BURSERACEAE (p. 113)
    36. Stamens 10 to 12 .... MELIACEAE (p. 117)
    36. Stamens 4 or 5 .... ANACARDIACEAE (p. 123)
37. Leaves entire or merely undulate 38
37. Leaves toothed or lobed 65
    38. Leaves with sheathing stipules ...... POLYGONACEAE (p. 61)
    38. Leaves without sheathing stipules 39
39. Sap milky 40
39. Sap clear 41
    40. Flowers borne inside a nearly closed, subspherical hollow ball or outside and arranged in a dense ball ...... MORACEAE (p. 51)
    40. Flowers not borne as above .... SAPOTACEAE (p. 171)
41. Leaves with an aniselike scent; fruit a whorl of free, spreading follicles .... ILLICIACEAE (p. 66)
41. Leaves and/or fruits not as above 42
    42. Leaves glandular-punctate below ..... MYRSINACEAE (p. 168)
    42. Leaves not glandular-punctate below 43
43. Leaves deciduous 44
43. Leaves evergreen 49
    44. Staminate flowers in catkins; fruit an acorn .FAGACEAE (p. 42)
    44. Staminate flowers not in catkins; fruit not an acorn 45
45. Leaves deeply bilobed at apex .... FABACEAE (p. 88)
45. Leaves not deeply bilobed at apex 46
    46. Leaves with a distinct spicelike odor when crushed, often irregularly lobed .... LAURACEAE (p. 69)
    46. Leaves without a distinct spicelike odor when crushed, never irregularly lobed 47
47. Stipules or stipular scars present .... ULMACEAE (p. 47)
47. Stipules or stipular scars absent 48
    48. Branches with a terminal bud .... NYSSACEAE (p. 160)
    48. Branches without a terminal bud .... EBENACEAE (p. 177)
49. Leaves with palmate veins 50
49. Leaves with pinnate veins 51
    50. Petiole enlarged at junction with leaf blade; fruit a legume .... FABACEAE (p. 88)
    50. Petiole not enlarged at junction with leaf blade; fruit a capsule .... MALVACEAE (p. 145)
51. Staminate flowers in catkins; fruit an acorn ...... FAGACEAE (p. 42)
51. Staminate flowers not in catkins; fruit not an acorn 52
    52. Branches spinescent .... OLACACEAE (p. 56)
    52. Branches not spinescent 53
53. Flowers 5 cm wide or over; fruit conelike .. MAGNOLIACEAE (p. 63)

53.	Flowers smaller than 5 cm wide; fruit not conelike	54
	54. Leaves with odor when crushed	55
	54. Leaves without an odor when crushed	56
55.	Fruit simple, 1-seeded LAURACEAE	(p. 69)
55.	Fruit compound, many-seeded ANNONACEAE	(p. 67)
	56. Leaves suborbicular, rounded or emarginate at apex CHRYSOBALANACEAE	(p. 85)
	56. Leaves other than suborbicular, acuminate to obtuse at apex	57
57.	Sap milky EUPHORBIACEAE	(p. 120)
57.	Sap clear	58
	58. Fruit dry	59
	58. Fruit fleshy	62
59.	Flowers or fruits in long axillary racemes CYRILLACEAE	(p. 126)
59.	Flowers or fruits in cymes, solitary, or few-flowered clusters	60
	60. Leaves gray green CELASTRACEAE	(p. 132)
	60. Leaves other than gray green	61
61.	Leaves congested towards ends of branches .SURIANACEAE	(p. 113)
61.	Leaves arranged more or less uniformly along the branches ERICACEAE	(p. 163)
	62. Flowers or fruits terminal	63
	62. Flowers or fruits axillary	64
63.	Fruit on a gynophore CAPPARACEAE	(p. 75)
63.	Fruit not on a gynophore ANACARDIACEAE	(p. 123)
	64. Fruit a drupe ROSACEAE	(p. 82)
	64. Fruit a berry AQUIFOLIACEAE	(p. 129)
65.	Leaves distinctly aromatic when crushed	66
65.	Leaves not distinctly aromatic when crushed	67
	66. Leaves irregularly toothed at apex MYRICACEAE	(p. 35)
	66. Leaves with 1 (rarely 2) large lobes, sometimes entire LAURACEAE	(p. 69)
67.	Leaves palmately lobed CARICACEAE	(p. 149)
67.	Leaves pinnately lobed or merely serrate	68
	68. Plants with milky sap MORACEAE	(p. 51)
	68. Plants without milky sap	69
69.	Flowers in catkins	70
69.	Flowers not in catkins	73
	70. Teeth on leaves irregular	71
	70. Teeth on leaves fairly uniform the whole length	72
71.	Fruit a drupe ULMACEAE	(p. 47)
71.	Fruit an acorn FAGACEAE	(p. 42)
	72. Leaf margins once-serrate SALICACEAE	(p. 35)
	72. Leaf margins twice-serrate BETULACEAE	(p. 40)
73.	Fruit a flat samara with notch at apex ULMACEAE	(p. 47)
73.	Fruit not as above	74

Key to Identification of Families **21**

	74.	Fruit an achene with a capillary pappus ASTERACEAE (p. 195)
	74.	Fruit other than above 75
75.		Fruit a dry capsule or nutlike 76
75.		Fruit a fleshy drupe, berry, or pome 79
	76.	Fruit nutlike ....TILIACEAE (p. 142)
	76.	Fruit a dry capsule 77
77.		Petals free 78
77.		Petals fused, at least part of their length ....ERICACEAE (p. 163)
	78.	Flowers over 3 cm wide ....THEACEAE (p. 145)
	78.	Flowers less than 3 cm wide .....HAMAMELIDACEAE (p. 78)
79.		Flowers or fruits axillary or axillary and terminal; leaves conspicuously scabrous above; flowers 4-5 cm long .....BORAGINACEAE (p. 184)
79.		Flowers or fruits all terminal; leaves smooth or nearly so above; flowers 1 cm long or less 80
	80.	Leaves pubescent on both surfaces, with conspicuous, adnate, persistent filiform stipules .......ELEOCARPACEAE (p. 142)
	80.	Leaves glabrous or nearly so above, various below, without conspicuous, adnate, persistent filiform stipules 81
81.		Flowers or fruits sessile or subsessile ....SYMPLOCACEAE (p. 177)
81.		Flowers or fruits distinctly pedicellate 82
	82.	Leaves with secondary veins parallel and distinct ....RHAMNACEAE (p. 139)
	82.	Leaves with secondary veins branching and often indistinct 83
83.		Twigs with horizontal lenticels ....ROSACEAE (p. 82)
83.		Twigs without horizontal lenticels 84
	84.	Ovary inferior ....ERICACEAE (p. 163)
	84.	Ovary superior ..................AQUIFOLIACEAE (p. 129)

Descriptive Flora

PINACEAE (Pine Family)

Trees or shrubs. Leaves evergreen, needlelike, spirally arranged, singly or in clusters. Flowers unisexual, borne on the same plant. Cones woody; seeds usually winged. 10 genera, about 250 species. Northern Hemisphere.

These important timber trees produce valuable forest products, such as tar, turpentine, rosin, pitch, cellophane, and plastics. The wood resists decay because of its high resin content.

PINUS (Pine)

Trees; stems and branches resinous. Leaves needlelike, in fascicles of 2 to 5 or rarely solitary; bud scales form a basal sheath. Staminate catkins produced at the ends of branches of the preceding year. Cones solitary or clustered, woody; seeds 2, winged. 70 to 100 species. Northern Hemisphere.

1. Needles in fascicles of 2 or sometimes 2 and 3 2
1. Needles in fascicles of 3 or sometimes of 3 and 4 3
    2. Needles 5-11 cm long; twigs smooth and slender; cones 5-8 cm long ....1. *P. clausa*
    2. Needles (12-) 20-25 cm long; twigs rough and stout; cones 8-16 cm long ....2. *P. elliottii*
3. Terminal bud silvery white ....3. *P. palustris*
3. Terminal bud rusty brown to chestnut brown 4
    4. Unopened cones subglobose to short-ovoid, 5-8 cm long 4. *P. serotina*
    4. Unopened cones elongate-ovoid (5-) 10-12 cm long .... .5. *P. taeda*

1. **Pinus clausa** (Engelm.) Sarg. (Sand Pine). Trees to 24 m tall: crown conical, moderately dense; branches slender, smooth; bark gray or brownish, relatively smooth. Leaves 5-11 cm long in clusters of 2, sheath about 5 mm long. Cones 5-8 cm long, scale faces with short stout spines. White sand oak-scrub community. Central peninsular Florida to southern Alabama. Spring. (Fig. 2)

24 TREES OF CENTRAL FLORIDA

Fig. 2. *Pinus clausa* (Sand Pine), × 2/5.

2. **Pinus elliottii** Engelm. (Slash Pine). Trees to 30 m tall; crown irregular, broadly conical; branches stout, brown; bark dark gray, furrowed, breaking into irregular plates. Leaves 18-30 cm long, in clusters of 2 or 3, sheath up to 1.5 cm long. Cones 8-15 cm long, scale faces reddish brown with a sharp, short prickle. Flatwoods. Throughout most of Florida to Louisiana and South Carolina. Spring.

Variety **densa** occurs with the typical form throughout the range of this manual and is more common to the south while var. **elliottii** is more common to the north. Once beyond the seedling stage, var. **densa** is not easily separated from the typical and is not distinguished here.

Slash pine is a high-quality timber tree.

3. **Pinus palustris** Mill. (Longleaf Pine). Trees to 40 m tall; crown cylindrical, open; branches rough, stout; terminal bud silvery white; bark grayish brown or reddish brown, thin scaly, furrowed. Leaves 20-45 cm long, in clusters of 3, sheath 2-3 cm long. Cones 15-25 cm long, scale faces keeled, with a short, curved prickle. Flatwoods and sandhill communities. Mid-Florida to Texas and Virginia. Spring. *Pinus australis* Michx. f.

Longleaf pine is one of the pitch pines and a valuable source of naval stores and lumber.

4. **Pinus serotina** Michx. (Pond Pine). Trees to 30 m tall; crown irregular, tufts of small branches and foliage often produced on trunks and main branches after being subjected to fire; branches slender and rough scaly; bark dark gray or reddish brown, forming irregular thin, narrow, vertical plates. Leaves 10-20 cm long, in clusters of 3 or 4, sheaths about 5 mm long. Cones 5-8 cm long, scale faces transversely keeled, each with a sharp incurved (often deciduous) spine; cones remain attached to the trees up to 12 years, and, as branches increase in size, the cones bcome imbedded in tissue and appear sessile. Poorly drained areas that are subject to frequent fires. North central part of Florida to Mississippi and New Jersey. Spring.

Both sand pine and pond pine have persistent closed cones. Sand pine, however, occurs in well-drained sites whereas pond pine occurs in poorly drained areas.

5. **Pinus taeda** L. (Loblolly Pine). Trees to 30 m or more tall; crown narrow to broadly conical; branches smooth, dull brown; bark gray, deeply furrowed, breaking into irregular plates. Leaves (10-) 17-23 (-25) cm long, in clusters of 3, sheath 0.5-1 cm long. Cones (5-) 10-13 cm long, scale faces transversely keeled, with a stout straight or recurved spine. Upland sites and old fields. Pasco and Orange counties northward, to Texas and New Jersey. Spring.

Loblolly pine yields lumber, although not of the best quality.

TAXODIACEAE (Bald Cypress Family)

Medium to large trees. Leaves scalelike or linear, spirally arranged, often twisting to a single plane. Flowers unisexual, borne on the same tree. Cones woody, globose, composed of angular, peltate scales; seeds irregular, angular. About 10 genera and 16 species. Eastern Asia, Tasmania, and North America.

26 TREES OF CENTRAL FLORIDA

TAXODIUM (Cypress)

Description as in family. 3 species. Southeastern United States and Mexico.

1. Leaves awl-shaped, appressed to twigs .... 1. *T. ascendens*
2. Leaves linear, spreading on twigs .... 2. *T. distichum*

Fig. 3. *Taxodium ascendens* (Pond Cypress), × 2/5.

1. **Taxodium ascendens** Brongn. (Pond Cypress). Trees to 30 m; crown pyramidal when young, later irregular; branches slender, smooth; bark gray to cinnamon brown, ridged, shredded, flaking. Leaves 8-10 mm long, awl-shaped, predominately keeled, margins incurved, appressed to branches. Cones globose, about 2.5 cm in diameter, scales angular, peltate; seeds angular, brown, 8-12 mm long. Flatwood ponds. Throughout Florida to Louisiana and Virginia. Spring. (Fig. 3)

This tree is sometimes considered a variety of the following species, in which case the name **Taxodium distichum** var. **nutans** (Ait.) Sweet is applied.

A characteristic growth feature of this and the following species are the buttressed bases of the trunks and outgrowths of the roots ("knees"). Pond cypress usually produces fewer knees than bald cypress, and the knees are blunt rather than pointed at the tips. The wood of pond cypress is equally as valuable for lumber as that of bald cypress because of its resistance to decay.

2. **Taxodium distichum** (L.) Rich. (Bald Cypress). Tree to 50 m; crown pyramidal when young, later irregular; branches slender, smooth; bark gray to cinnamon brown, ridged, shredded, flaking. Leaves 10-15 mm long, narrowly lanceolate, tips acute, margin flat, entire. Cones globose, about 2.5 cm in diameter, scales angular, peltate; seeds angular, brown, 8-12 mm long. Swamps and floodplains. Throughout Florida to Texas, Delaware, and up the Mississippi Valley to southern Illinois and Indiana. Spring.

This species is a commercially valuable tree so virgin stands are extremely rare.

CUPRESSACEAE (Cypress Family)

Trees or shrubs. Leaves evergreen, scalelike or awl-shaped, decurrent, whorled or opposite. Flowers unisexual, borne on the same or different plants. Cones woody, leathery, or berrylike; seeds winged or unwinged. 19 genera, about 130 species. Cosmopolitan.

1. Twigs flattened when viewed in cross-section;
   cones woody, brown .... 1. *Chamaecyparis*
1. Twigs quadrangular when viewed in cross-section;
   cones berrylike, blue .... 2. *Juniperus*

1. CHAMAECYPARIS (False Cypress)

Trees with spreading branches; branchlets numerous from axils of lateral leaves, forming a flat spray. Leaves scalelike, imbricate, opposite, each with a gland on back. Flowers unisexual, borne on the same plant. Cones woody, the scales peltate; seeds small, winged. 7 species. North America and Asia.

1. **Chamaecyparis thyoides** (L.) BSP (Atlantic White Cedar). Characters of the genus. In swamps or along streams in woods. Rare in the range of this manual, known only from Marion County. North to Mississippi and Maine. Spring. (Fig. 4)

All *Chamaecyparis* yield good and useful timber.

JUNIPERUS (Juniper)

Trees or shrubs; bark reddish brown, exfoliating. Leaves evergreen, scalelike or awllike, imbricate, whorled, each with a translucent gland on the back. Flowers unisexual, borne on the same plant. Cones subglobose, berrylike, blue, glaucous; seeds wingless. 60 species. Northern Hemisphere.

1. **Juniperus silicicola** (Small) Bailey (Southern Red Cedar). Characters of the genus. Old fields, open woods, coastal hammocks, beaches, and Indian shell mounds. Throughout Florida to New Mexico and North Carolina. Spring. *Sabina silicicola* Small. (Fig. 5)

ARECACEAE (Palm Family)

Medium to large trees with solitary terminal bud; trunks unbranched, crowned with leaves. Leaf blades plaited, pinnate or palmate. Flowers bisexual or unisexual, 3-parted, borne on spadix subtended by a woody spathe, stamens 6 to 12; pistils 3; carpels free or united. Fruit drupaceous or baccate. About 217 genera, 2500 species. Tropical and warm temperate regions.

1. Leaves costapalmate .... 1. *Sabal*
1. Leaves palmate .... 2. *Washingtonia*

1. SABAL (Sabal)

Tree to 20 meters; crown globose. Leaves costapalmate, long petioled, blades arching, margins longer than the midvein, strongly filiferous. 25 species. Warmer America, West Indies.

1. **Sabal palmetto** (Walt.) Lodd. ex Schultes (Cabbage Palm). Trees to 10 m tall or more, erect. Leaves costapalmate, petioles two-

Fig. 4. *Chamaecyparis thyoides* (Atlantic White Cedar), × 1/2.

Fig. 5. *Juniperus silicicola* (Southern Red Cedar), × 7/10.

Descriptive Flora 31

Fig. 6. *Sabal palmetto* (Cabbage Palm), × 2/5.

edged, unarmed, narrowed and extended into the downward curving blade; sinuses filiferous. Flowers bisexual, fragrant, white, about 3 mm long, borne in a long spadix. Fruit a globose drupe, to 9 mm in diameter, edible. Wet or dry habitats, salt and mineral waters, coastal hammocks, and glades. Throughout Florida to Alabama and North Carolina. Spring. (Fig. 6)

Cabbage palm, the most common native arborescent palm in Florida, is the state tree. Frequently used for ornamental planting, it has provided man with food (fruits and heart of palm) and shelter.

2. WASHINGTONIA (Washington Palm)

Tree to 30 m or more tall, erect. Leaf blades plicate, deeply cut, filiferous; petioles armed with hooked, yellow spines; vernation infolded. Flowers bisexual, white, perianth toothed; stamens 6; ovary 3-lobed. Fruits black, small, ellipsoid drupes. 2 species. Arizona, California, and Baja, California. (Fig. 7)

1. **Washingtonia robusta** Wendl. (Desert Palm). Characters of the genus. Naturalized in disturbed sites along the Gulf coast of Florida. Native in southwestern states. Spring.

CASUARINACEAE (Beefwood Family)

Trees or shrubs with whorled jointed branches, resembling a conifer. Leaves evergreen, reduced to toothed or scalelike whorls or sheaths surrounding nodes of branches. Flowers unisexual, on same or different trees; staminate flowers spicate in sheaths toward end of branches; pistillate flowers in dense spherical or ovoid heads becoming woody and conelike. Fruit a 1-seeded nut with terminal wings. 2 genera, 65 species. Australia and southeast Asia.

CASUARINA (Beefwood)

Characters of family. 40 species. Australia and Southeast Asia.

1. Scales (leaves) 6 to 8 per whorl ....1. *C. litorea*
1. Scales (leaves) 12 to 16 per whorl ....2. *C. glauca*

1. **Casuarina litorea** L. (Australian Pine). Shrubs or trees to 40 m with open slender branches. Leaves 6 to 8 per whorl, 1-3 mm long on dark green "needles" that are jointed branches. Staminate spikes 1-5 cm long; pistillate spikes globular, 1-2 cm wide in fruit. Fruit conelike and woody. Naturalized in sandy shores and pinelands in coastal counties. Spring. *C. equisetifolia* L. (Fig. 8)

Fig. 7. *Washingtonia robusta* (Desert Palm), × 1/6.

Australian pine is planted as an ornamental or windbreak in parks, along canals, and roads. The roots have nitrogen-fixing nodules. The timber is immune to termites. The bark yields yellow dye and tannin. The wood burns without being dried.

2. **Casuarina glauca** Sieber ex Spreng. (Suckering Australian Pine). Shrubs or trees up to 20 m with dense bushy branches. Leaves 12 to 16 per whorl, branches (needles) glossy green. Staminate flowers in terminal spikes 1-3 cm long. Fields and open woods. Southern counties. Spring.

This species is widely planted as an ornamental and occasionally escapes and becomes naturalized.

Fig. 8. *Casuarina litorea* (Australian Pine), × 1/3.

SALICACEAE (Willow Family)

Trees and shrubs. Leaves alternate, stipulate. Flowers unisexual on different plants, borne in catkins, each flower subtended by a bract; perianth lacking; stamens 1 to 12; pistils compound, stigmas 2; ovary 1-locular. Seeds comate with silky hair. 3 genera, 350 species. North temperate regions.

SALIX (Willow)

Trees or shrubs; lateral buds with a single bud scale. Leaves narrowly lanceolate or oblanceolate; stipules often prominent. Catkins erect to ascending, scales commonly hairy with nectar glands at bases of filaments and pistils. Capsules dehisce by two recurving valves. 200 species. North temperate regions.

1. Mature leaves lanceolate, glaucous below . . . . .1. *S. caroliniana*
1. Mature leaves elliptic-oblong, soft pubescent below . . . . .2. *S. floridana*

1. **Salix caroliniana** Michx. (Carolina Willow). Trees to 19 m tall, sometimes with more than one trunk from extended rootstocks; branches slender, pliable, yellowish green becoming reddish gray at maturity; older bark furrowed and checkered, gray on ridges. Leaves lustrous, green above, glaucous below, margins yellowish, usually glandular-serrulate. Catkins 7-10 cm long, somewhat drooping, bracts densely pubescent. Moist soil, canal banks, and ditches. Throughout Florida to Texas, Maryland, and Kansas. Spring. *S. amphibia* Small; *S. longipes* Anders.; *S. marginata* Wim. (Fig. 9)

2. **Salix floridana** Chapm. (Florida Willow). Shrub or small tree. Leaves oval or broadly elliptic-oblong, bases broadly rounded, 12-15 cm long and 5 cm wide; upper surfaces dark green and glabrous, lower surfaces white soft pubescent. Flowers in catkins. Wet woodlands, along small streams. A rare willow; Lake, Levy, and Marion counties in central Florida. Spring.

MYRICACEAE (Bayberry Family)

Aromatic trees or shrubs. Leaves evergreen, simple, alternate, resin-dotted, with or without stipules. Flowers unisexual, on same or different plants; borne in catkins, rising from lateral scaly buds; involucre and perianth lacking. Fruit a waxy drupe. 3 genera, 50 species. Cosmopolitan.

Fig. 9. *Salix caroliniana* (Carolina Willow), × 1/2.

MYRICA (Bayberry)

Shrub or low trees. Leaves entire or irregularly toothed. Flowers unisexual, on same or different plants; staminate catkins bristly, cylindric; stamens 2 to many, subtended by a hooded bract; pistillate catkins not so conspicuously bracteate; ovary subtended by 2 to 4 bracts. Fruit a globular drupe in clusterlike spikes, waxy. 35 species. Nearly cosmopolitan.

1. **Myrica cerifera** L. (Wax Myrtle). Bushy trees to 6 m tall. Leaves

Fig. 10. *Myrica cerifera* (Wax Myrtle), × 3/5.

oblong-cuneate to 9 cm long, toothed at apex, reduced toward tips of branches, fragrant, resinous. Fruit a globose drupe, 2-3 mm in diameter, waxy with bloom. Hammocks, wet sandy soil and swamps. Throughout Florida to Texas and Arkansas. Winter. *Cerothamnus ceriferus* (L.) Small; *Cerothamnus caroliniensis* (Mill.) Tidest.; *Cerothamnus pumilus* (Michx.) Small; *Myrica pusilla* Raf. (Fig. 10)

The waxy coat of the wax myrtle fruit is used to make fragrant candles.

JUGLANDACEAE (Walnut Family)

Trees or shrubs. Leaves deciduous, alternate, odd-pinnate. Flowers unisexual, on same plants; staminate flowers in catkins; pistillate flowers in erect spikes, calyx 1- to 4-lobed, ovary inferior. Fruit a nut, covered with a husk splitting into 4 valves or indehiscent. 6 genera, about 50 species. North temperate and subtropical regions.

CARYA (Hickory)

Trees. Staminate flowers in pendulous, 3-branched catkins; pistillate flowers solitary or clustered, terminating the branches. Fruit a hard-shelled nut enclosed by a 4-valved husk. About 18 species. Eastern North America.

Hickories furnish a durable wood. The nuts are a source of food for wildlife and man.

1. Leaflets 9 to 15 2
1. Leaflets 5 to 7 3
   2. Rachis and lower surface of leaflets puberulent ......1. *C. aquatica*
   2. Rachis and lower surface of leaflets glabrous ......4. *C. illinoensis*
3. Outer bud scales (except sometimes terminal and subterminal on older branches) completely enclosing inner, with conspicuous yellow lepidote scales; plant of sand-pine scrub ....2. *C. floridana*
3. Outer bud scales soon splitting and exposing conspicuously hairy inner; yellow lepidote scales absent or inconspicuous; plants of dry to moist deciduous woods ....3. *C. glabra*

1. **Carya aquatica** (Michx. f.) Nutt. (Water Hickory). Trees to 25 m tall; crown of upright branches; bark light or dark gray, rough and deeply furrowed. Leaflets 9 to 15, scythe-shaped, thin, tomentum persisting in leaf axils. Fruits to 3 cm long, 4-angled, husk dehiscent to middle. Swamp forests. Nearly throughout Florida to Texas, Mississippi, and Missouri. Spring. *Hicoria aquatica* (Michx. f.) Britt. (Fig. 11)

2. **Carya floridana** Sarg. (Scrub Hickory). Trees to 20 m tall,

Fig. 11. *Carya aquatica* (Water Hickory), × 1/2.

usually small tree in scrub formations; crown rounded of slender leafy branches; bark pale greenish gray, furrows obscure. Leaflets 3 to 5, rarely 7, lanceolate, oblanceolate, acuminate, narrowed to sessile base; marginal teeth serrate. Fruits to 3 cm long, husk tardily separating; nut rusty, scaly, becoming glabrous. Sand-pine scrub. Nearly throughout. Endemic to Florida. Spring. *Hicoria floridana* (Sarg.) Small

3. **Carya glabra** (Mill.) Sweet (Pignut Hickory). Tree to 20 m tall; crown irregularly open; bark with prominent interlacing ridges. Leaflets 5 to 7, terminal leaflet the largest, broadly oblanceolate to obovate. Fruit an obovoid, stalked nut; husk dehiscent part way to base. Dry to moist woods. Nearly throughout except for southernmost counties. North to Texas, Michigan, and Vermont. Spring. *Hicoria glabra* (Mill.) Britt.

4. **Carya illinoensis** (Wang.) K. Koch (Pecan). Tree to 50 m tall; bark somewhat roughened. Leaflets 9 to 15, oblong-lanceolate, the laterals conspicuously scythe-shaped, the terminal on a stalk 2-4 cm long. Fruits ovoid or ellipsoid about 4 cm long, the sutures of the husks prominently winged, splitting the entire length; nut ellipsoid, smooth, thin-shelled. Disturbed thickets; escaped from cultivation in our area. Native in Northern Florida to Alabama, Texas, and Iowa. Spring. *Hicoria pecan* (Marsh.) Britt.

The kernel is edible and is used extensively for food.

BETULACEAE (Birch Family)

Trees or shrubs. Leaves simple, alternate, serrate. Flowers unisexual, on same plant; staminate catkins drooping, with each bract subtending two or three flowers, calyx present; pistillate catkins seldom drooping, the bracts woody, each bearing 2 or 3 pistils, the calyx wanting. Fruit conelike or aggregate of accrescent bracts, each subtending or enclosing 1 to 3 nutlets. 6 genera, about 137 species. North temperate and tropical montane areas.

1. Fruit a nut subtended by a 3-lobed leafy bract, bark smooth, blue gray . . . . 1. *Carpinus*
1. Fruit a nut enclosed in a papery sac; bark shredded, reddish brown . . . . 2. *Ostrya*

1. CARPINUS (Hornbeam)

Trees or shrubs to 10 m tall; bark smooth. Leaves alternate, serrate. Staminate catkins in clusters of 3, in axils of winter bud scales;

stamens 2 or more without perianth, adnate to bract; pistillate flowers in a cluster of 2 or more; 2 styles; inferior ovary subtended by foliaceous involucre. Fruit a 1-sided nutlet with a 3-lobed leafy wing on one side. 35 species. Northern Hemisphere.

1. **Carpinus caroliniana** Walt. (American Hornbeam). Characters of genus. Wet woods and swamps. Central Florida to Texas, Minnesota, and northeastern United States. Spring–summer. (Fig. 12)

The wood is used for tool handles.

Fig. 12. *Carpinus caroliniana* (American Hornbeam), × 7/10.

2. OSTRYA (Hop Hornbeam)

Shrubs or trees with scaly bark. Leaves alternate, serrate. Staminate catkins usually clustered with close imbricate bracts; pistillate catkins with lobeless bracts; calyx minute; ovary inferior. Bracts become enlarged to form a hoplike strobilus enclosing flattened, ovoid nutlets. 10 species. North temperate zone.

1. **Ostrya virginiana** (Mill.) K. Koch (Hop Hornbeam). Characters of genus. Hammocks and well-drained floodplains. Middle Florida to Texas and Maine. Spring–summer. (Fig. 13)

FAGACEAE (Beech Family)

Trees or shrubs. Leaves simple, alternate, deciduous or evergreen. Flowers unisexual, on same plant; staminate numerous in catkinlike or erect spikes, calyx with 4 to 6 lobes, stamens few to many; pistillate solitary or in small clusters on short spikes, calyx with 4 to 6 lobes, styles 3, ovary inferior. Fruit a nut enclosed or partly enclosed by an involucre or cup of wholly or partly fused, hardened bracts. 8 genera, 900 species. Widely distributed in tropical, subtropical, and temperate regions.

1. QUERCUS (Oak)

Trees or shrubs. Leaves deciduous or evergreen, often lobed, cleft or parted, margins serrate, crenate or entire, lobes or teeth with or without bristles. Staminate flowers in clustered, drooping catkins, calyx 2- to 8-lobed, stamens 3 to 12; pistillate flowers in short spikes or solitary, calyx 6-lobed. Nut partially enclosed by cupule, forming the acorn. 450 species. Tropical, subtropical, and temperate regions.

1. Leaves mostly conspicuously lobed to about halfway to midrib 2
1. Leaves shallowly lobed or entire 4
   2. Leaves bristle-tipped 3
   2. Leaves not bristle-tipped ....11. *Q. stellata*
3. Leaves with truncate to broadly cuneate bases, sinuses deep, rounded; acorn cup covering less than one-third of acorn .....10. *Q. shumardii*
3. Leaves with gradually cuneate bases, sinuses broad, open; acorn cup covering one-third or more of acorn ....5. *Q. laevis*
   4. Leaf margins regularly dentate ....7. *Q. michauxii*
   4. Leaf margins entire or irregularly few-toothed 5
5. Leaves mostly shallowly 3-lobed and broadest at apex 6
5. Leaves never 3-lobed at apex and broadest near middle 7
   6. Leaves bristle-tipped ....9. *Q. nigra*

Descriptive Flora 43

Fig. 13. *Ostrya virginiana* (Hop Hornbeam), × 2/5.

6. Leaves not bristle-tipped ....2. *Q durandii*
7. Leaves revolute 8
7. Leaves not revolute 9
   8. Leaves usually oblong, rugose above, densely gray pubescent below at maturity ....3. *Q. geminata*
   8. Leaves broadly elliptic to oval, smooth above, glabrate below at maturity ....8. *Q. myrtifolia*
9. Leaves finely, but densely tomentose below 10
9. Leaves glabrous, sparsely pubescent, or pubescent only in vein axils below 11
   10. Leaves bluish or shiny green; inner surface of nut shell glabrous ....4. *Q incana*
   10. Leaves dark green; inner surface of nut shell pubescent ....12. *Q. virginiana*
11. Leaves usually broadly elliptic to obovate, broadly rounded at base, rusty pubescent below; inner surface of nut shell glabrous ....1. *Q. chapmanii*
11. Leaves usually narrowly obovate, cuneate at base, glabrous below; inner surface of nut shell pubescent ....6. *Q. laurifolia*

    1. **Quercus chapmanii** Sarg. (Chapman Oak). Small tree or shrub; bark broken into irregular plates. Leaves persisting until spring, obovate to elliptic, 5-10 cm long, unlobed or indistinctly 3-lobed, tips rounded, bases cuneate to rounded, margins entire, undulate, glabrous and nonlustrous above, sparsely pubescent below. Acorn sessile, solitary or paired; cup hemispheric, enclosing one-third to one-half the nut. Pine flatwoods. Broward County northward to South Carolina. Spring.

    2. **Quercus durandii** Buckl. (Bluff Oak). Tree up to 25 m tall; bark pale gray, scaly or shaggy. Leaves deciduous, simple, green and shiny above, paler beneath, 5-15 cm long; oblong-ovate, tips rounded, bases rounded or cuneate, lobes 5 to 7, upper lobes pointing forward. Acorns sessile or short-peduncled, annual, ovoid; cups thin, enclosing one-third to one-half the nut, covered with thin, blunt, overlapping scales. Wooded slopes and stream banks. Marion County northward to Georgia, Texas, Arkansas. Spring. *Quercus austrina* Small

    3. **Quercus geminata** Small (Sand Live Oak). Small to medium-sized tree; bark thick, roughly ridged and furrowed. Leaves persisting until spring, simple, thick, leathery, strongly revolute, coarsely veined and densely tomentose beneath, 3-6 cm long. Acorns annual, ovoid, paired on distinct peduncles; cups turbinate, enclosing one-third the length of nut. Sandhills, oak scrubland, and coastal dunes. DeSoto

County northward to Mississippi and North Carolina. Spring. *Quercus virginiana* var. *geminata* Sarg.

4. **Quercus incana** Bartr. (Bluejack Oak). Small tree or shrub; bark dark gray to black, deeply corrugated. Leaves deciduous, elliptic to oblanceolate, 5-12 cm long, entire, apices tipped with a short bristle; leaves silvery tomentose below, upper surface becoming bluish at maturity. Acorns, subglobose, nearly sessile; cup shallow, saucer-shaped, enclosing one-fourth the nut, scales blunt, pale-pubescent. Sandhills. Lee County northward to Texas, Oklahoma, and North Carolina. Spring. *Quercus cinera* Michx.

5. **Quercus laevis** Walt. (Turkey Oak). Tree to 15 m tall; bark thick, deeply furrowed, blackish. Leaves deciduous, 10-20 cm long, simple, green and shiny above, red in fall, margins with 3 to 7 lobes, bases long-cuneate. Acorn 20-25 mm long, nut ovoid; cup enclosing one-third to one-half the nut, scales incurved, pubescent. Sandhills and dry pinelands. Sarasota and Martin counties northward to Louisiana and Virginia. Spring.

6. **Quercus laurifolia** Michx. (Laurel Oak). Trees up to 30 m tall; bark dark, scaly. Leaves tardily deciduous, elliptic, broadest above the middle, tapered at both ends, occasionally 3-lobed at apex, occasionally bristle-tipped, shiny green above, duller below, 4-12 cm long. Acorn sessile or nearly so, broadly ovoid; cup shallow, covering about one-fourth of nut. Wet woods and mesic oak-pinelands. Throughout Florida to Louisiana and Virginia. Spring. *Quercus obtusa* (Willd.) Pursh.

7. **Quercus michauxii** Nutt. (Swamp Chestnut Oak). Tree up to 25 m tall; bark pale gray, shaggy. Leaves deciduous, simple, obovate or oval, 8-16 cm long, coarsely crenate-serrate, tomentose beneath. Acorns ovoid to subcylindric, sessile or short-peduncled, paired or solitary. Mesic hammocks and lime sinks. Hernando County northward to Texas, Missouri, and New Jersey. Spring. *Quercus prinus* L.

8. **Quercus myrtifolia** Willd. (Myrtle Oak). Scrubby tree or shrub; bark light gray, smooth, becoming shallowly furrowed near base of trunk. Leaves evergreen, 2-6 cm long, ovate to obovate, apices rounded, bases rounded to broadly cuneate, margins entire, revolute. Acorns solitary or paired, ovoid to subglobose; cup bowl-shaped, enclosing about one-fourth of nut, scales small, appressed. Sandhills, oak scrub, and pine flatwoods. Broward County northward to Mississippi and South Carolina. Spring.

9. **Quercus nigra** L. (Water Oak). Tree to 25 m tall; bark smooth,

becoming shallowly and irregularly furrowed. Leaves tardily deciduous, spatulate to obovate, 5-14 cm long, with 3 terminal lobes, the lobes bristle-tipped, both surfaces glabrous, green. Acorns single or in pairs, sessile or short-peduncled, ovoid to hemispheric, 1-1.5 cm long; cup shallowly saucerlike. Wet woods and mesic oak–pine woodlands. Manatee County northward to Texas, Missouri, and Delaware. Spring. (Fig. 14)

10. **Quercus shumardii** Buckl. (Shumard Oak). Tree to 35 m tall;

Fig. 14. *Quercus nigra* (Water Oak), × 3/5.

bark thick with deep fissures, gray scaly ridges. Leaves deciduous, 6-20 cm long, 7 to 9 deep lobes with 3 to 13 secondary bristle-tipped lobes, bases truncate to broadly cuneate, shiny green above, paler below. Acorn solitary or in pairs, subsessile, oblong to ovoid, 1.5-2 cm long; cups thick, shallow, saucerlike, enclosing one-third the nut, scales tuberculate, closely appressed. Wet woods and hammocks. Citrus County northward to Texas, Iowa, and North Carolina. Spring.

11. **Quercus stellata** Wang. (Post Oak). Trees to 20 m tall; bark on older trunks broken by deep fissures into flat, loose scales; twigs and petioles tomentose. Leaves deciduous, 10-20 cm long, broadly obovate, cuneate at base, 5-lobed, the upper lobes much the larger, squarish, upper surface dark green and rough, lower surface tomentose with gray-brown stellate hairs. Acorns single or clustered, subsessile, oval, 12-14 mm long; cup enclosing one-third the nut, scales thin, closely appressed. Oak–pine woodlands. Citrus County northward to Texas, Nebraska, and Massachusetts. Spring.

Quercus stellata var. **margaretta** (Ashe) Sarg. extends to Pinellas and Polk counties. The leaves have 3 to 5 shallow lobes.

12. **Quercus virginiana** Mill. (Live Oak). Tree to 16 m tall; trunk to 1 m in diameter; crown spreading up to 35 m; bark dark gray, thick, roughly ridged and furrowed. Leaves evergreen, simple, dark shiny green above, paler, densely pubescent below, oblong or elliptic, 4-12 cm long, entire, revolute. Acorn solitary or in clusters, pedunculate, oblong to ovoid, 20-25 mm long, nearly black; cup turbinate, enclosing one-third of the nut. Hammocks and dry to wet woods. Throughout Florida to Texas and Virginia. Spring.

ULMACEAE (Elm Family)

Trees. Leaves alternate, deciduous, singly or doubly serrate or entire. Flowers unisexual, on same or different plants; inconspicuous in fascicles or cymes, or solitary; corolla none; calyx 4- to 9-parted with as many stamens opposite the lobes; ovary superior. Fruit a samara, nut, or drupe. About 15 genera, 200 species. Temperate and tropical areas.

1. Fruit a samara ....3. *Ulmus*
1. Fruit a drupe 2
   2. Leaves pubescent below; flowers in branching cymes ......2. *Trema*
   2. Leaves glabrous or with few appressed hairs below;
      flowers solitary or in few-flowered clusters ....1. *Celtis*

1. CELTIS (Hackberry)

Trees to 30 m tall; bark often warty. Leaves deciduous, lanceolate, asymmetrical margins entire or singly serrate. Flowers small, solitary or rarely paired in leaf axils, lower 2 to 5 flowers staminate, the upper pistillate; calyx 5- to 6-lobed; stamens 5 to 6; ovary ovoid; style short with 2 elongate, subulate, recurved stigmas. Fruit a subglobose drupe, purple, yellow, or orange. About 80 species. Northern Hemisphere and Africa.

1. Branches with short spines; flowers and fruits few in cymes 2
1. Branches unarmed; flowers and fruits solitary ....2. *C. laevigata*
    2. Leaves crenulate-dentate, somewhat succulent, upper surface decidedly scabrous ....3. *C. pallida*
    2. Leaves serrulate, chartaceous, upper surface smooth or nearly so ....1. *C. iguanaea*

1. **Celtis iguanaea** (Jacq.) Sarg. (Chaparral Shrub). Shrub or small tree; branches with recurved spines, glabrous. Leaf blades ovate or elliptic-ovate, 4-12 cm long, coarsely toothed. Calyx rotate, the lobes much longer than the tube; stigmas 2, each 2-cleft. Fruit a globose-ovoid drupe, 8-12 mm in diameter. Shell mounds. Southwest coast of Florida, Texas, and Mexico. Spring. *Momisia iguanaea* (Jacq.) Rose & Standl.

2. **Celtis laevigata** Willd. (Hackberry). Trees up to 30 m tall, usually with corky outgrowths. Leaves 6-12 cm long, lance-ovate to ovate, entire or serrate, often long tapering, oblique to the base. Flowers small, greenish, unisexual; staminate flowers with 5 to 6 stamens. Drupe 5-7 mm wide, globose, reddish brown or orange red. Wet woods. Nearly throughout Florida to Texas, Missouri, and New Jersey. Spring. *Celtis mississippiensis* Bosc.; *Celtis smallii* Beadle (Fig. 15)

The wood of the hackberry is used for crating, furniture, and cooperage.

3. **Celtis pallida** Torr. (Chaparral Shrub). Tree, stem and branches spreading; branches puberulent, with straight spines. Leaf blades ovate to elliptic, 2-3.5 cm long, coarsely toothed, scabrous. Fruit a subglobose drupe, 5-8 mm in diameter. Shell mounds. Southwest coast of Florida, Texas, and Mexico. Spring. *Momisia pallida* (Torr.) Planch.

2. TREMA

Trees and shrubs with smooth bark. Leaves oblique, serrate, persistent. Flowers polygamous in axillary cymes; calyx rotate, 5-parted, lobes exceeding the tube; stigmas 2; ovary superior. Fruit a

Fig. 15. *Celtis laevigata* (Hackberry), × 1/2.

drupe surrounded by persistent perianth. About 30 species. Tropics and subtropics.

1. **Trema micranthum** (L.) Blume (Nettle Tree). Characters of the genus. Edges of hammocks, thickets. Southern Florida, West Indies, and tropical America. All year. *Trema floridanum* Britt. (Fig. 16)

3. ULMUS (Elm)

Shrubs or trees; bark furrowed; branches sometimes winged. Leaves alternate, simple, short-petioled or subsessile, base unequal, usually doubly serrate. Flowers bisexual, in fascicles or racemes; calyx campanulate, 4- to 9-lobed or cleft; stamens as many as calyx seg-

50 TREES OF CENTRAL FLORIDA

Fig. 16. *Trema micranthum* (Nettle Tree), × 3/5.

ments, exserted; styles 2, short. Fruit a flat, 1-seeded stipitate samara. 45 species. Northern Hemisphere, Mexico, and tropical Asia.

The bark fibers have been fabricated into twine and cloth, and the bark yields medicinal materials.

1. Twigs corky winged 2
1. Twigs not corky winged ....2. *U. americana*
    2. Leaves acute to rounded at apex, decidedly scabrous above; calyx greenish, 6- to 9-lobed; plant flowering in fall . .3. *U. crassifolia*
    2. Leaves acuminate at apex, smooth or nearly so above; calyx yellowish red, 5-lobed; plants flowering in spring ....1. *U. alata*

Descriptive Flora 51

1. **Ulmus alata** Michx. (Winged Elm). Tree to 20 m tall; branches often corky winged. Leaves oblong or obovate, 4-7 cm long, typically smooth above. Flowers in racemes up to 1 cm long, calyx deeply lobed. Samaras narrowly obovate, about 1 cm long including the stipe, ciliate, pubescent on the sides. Dry to mesic woods. Osceola County northward to Texas, Kansas, Indiana, and Virginia. Spring.

2. **Ulmus americana** L. (American Elm). Tree up to 30 m tall; twigs smooth to short pubescent. Leaves elliptic, oval or ovate, 3-12 cm long, doubly serrate, smooth above, petioles 6-10 mm long. Flowers fascicled, on pedicels of unequal length up to 2 cm; calyx shallowly lobed, oblique. Samaras elliptic, notched at apex, about 1 cm long, densely ciliate, sides glabrous. Wet woods. Northern two-thirds of Florida to Texas, Michigan, and Maine. Spring. *Ulmus floridana* Chapm. (Fig. 17)

3. **Ulmus crassifolia** Nutt. (Cedar Elm). Tree to 30 m tall; branches often corky winged; twigs pubescent. Leaves 1.5-4 cm long, elliptic to ovate, apex obtuse, finely serrate, rough above; petioles 1-2 mm long. Samaras oval, ciliate, 8-10 mm long. Wet woods. Hernando County northward to Texas and Arkansas.

MORACEAE (Mulberry Family)

Trees or shrubs with milky juice. Leaves deciduous, mostly alternate, simple or palmately lobed, serrate. Flowers unisexual, on same or different plants; small, green, often in heads, cymes, umbels, or hollow receptacles; stamens 1 to 2; pistil 1; ovary superior. Fruit an achene or drupelike, more often a multiple fruit from the fusion of fruits from several flowers. 53 genera and 1400 species. Tropical and subtropical regions.

1. Leaf margins entire (leaves sometimes palmately 3- to 5-lobed) 2
1. Leaf margins serrate or dentate 3
   2. Staminate and pistillate flowers on inside of receptacle; fruit up to 2.5 cm wide; leaves coriaceous ....2. *Ficus*
   2. Staminate and pistillate flowers on outside of receptacle; fruit 5-15 cm in diameter; leaves papery ....3. *Maclura*
3. Pistillate inflorescence globose; stigma solitary ....1. *Broussonetia*
3. Pistillate inflorescence cylindrical; stigmas 2 ....4. *Morus*

1. BROUSSONETIA (Paper Mulberry)

Shrub or small tree to 15 m tall, stoloniferous; crown spreading, lower branches pendulous; bark smooth; young twigs and petioles

52 TREES OF CENTRAL FLORIDA

Fig. 17. *Ulmus americana* (American Elm), × 1/2.

hirsute. Leaves alternate, deciduous, blades serrate, often lobed, scabrous above, velvety pubescent beneath; stipules to 1.5 cm long, early deciduous. Flowers unisexual, on different plants; staminate flowers in catkins, sepals 4, stamens 4; pistillate flowers in globose clusters, calyx 4-lobed. Fruit multiple, globular, each achene protruding from persistent calyx. 7 or 8 species. East Asia.

1. **Broussonetia papyrifera** (L.) Vent. (Paper Mulberry). Characters of genus. Disturbed sites. Northern half of Florida to Missouri and New York. Introduced Asiatic tree, escaped from cultivation. Spring. *Papyrius papyrifera* (L.) Kuntze (Fig. 18)

The inner bark furnishes paper and tapa cloth.

2. FICUS (Fig)

Shrubs, trees, or vines with smooth bark. Leaves alternate, entire or lobed, pinnately veined, usually persistent. Flowers unisexual, sessile, axillary inside a hollow, globose receptacle; staminate flowers with 1 to 2 stamens. Multiple fruit, elongate or globular, achenes enclosed. 800 species. Tropics and subtropics.

1. Fruits sessile or subsessile . . . . .1. *F. aurea*
1. Fruits peduncled . . . . .2. *F. citrifolia*

1. **Ficus aurea** Nutt. (Strangler Fig). Tree to 20 m tall, often starting as an epiphyte, then a vine or treelike; twigs glabrous; bark gray green with prominent lenticels. Leaves elliptic or oval, pinnately veined, margins entire. Fruit sessile, spherical or obovoid, to 2 cm diameter, red or brown. Hammocks. Middle Florida southward to West Indies. All year. (Fig. 19)

A seed of the strangler fig tree, germinating in the bark of a hammock tree, develops into an epiphytal seedling. As it grows, a large number of aerial roots are produced. These, on reaching the ground, develop an underground root system sending forth numerous aerial shoots, which envelop and coalesce and eventually strangle the support tree. Subsequently, the shoots arise as a terrestrial forest tree.

2. **Ficus citrifolia** Mill. (Shortleaf Fig). Tree to 12 m tall; twigs glabrous. Leaves elliptic or ovate, 5-10 cm long, glabrous, rounded or cordate at base; peduncle 1-2 cm long. Hammocks. Rare in central Florida. South Florida, West Indies to South America. Spring–summer. *Ficus brevifolia* Nutt.

Ficus carica L. (Common Fig), a small tree with pubescent leaves,

Fig. 18. *Broussonetia papyrifera* (Paper Mulberry), × 3/5.

Fig. 19. *Ficus aurea* (Strangler Fig), × 1/2.

3- to 5-lobed, is sometimes encountered as persistent from cultivation. It is the common edible fig.

3. MACLURA (Osage Orange)

Shrub or tree to 20 m tall; spiny. Leaves alternate, ovate-lanceolate, 4-30 cm long, acuminate, dark green and lustrous above, simple, entire. Flowers on different plants; staminate flowers in spherical clusters 1-1.5 cm long, on short spur branches; pistillate in axillary, spherical clusters about 3 cm long. Fruit with milky juice, green, 1 dm in diameter; achenes deeply imbedded. 12 species. Warm regions.

1. **Maclura pomifera** (Raf.) Schneid. (Osage Orange). Characters of genus. Thickets. Rare in Florida. Texas, Georgia, and Missouri. Spring. *Toxylon pomiferum* Raf. (Fig. 20)

4. MORUS (Mulberry)

Trees or shrubs; bark smooth or scaly. Leaves alternate, variously lobed or unlobed, crenate. Flowers unisexual, on same or different plants; staminate flowers arranged in loose spikes, sepals 4, stamens 4; pistillate in dense spikes, sepals 4, pistil 2-parted. Fruit of multiple nutlets, each surrounded by fleshy calyx. 10 species. Chiefly north temperate.

1. Leaf blades glabrous below .... 1. *M. alba*
1. Leaf blades pubescent below .... 2. *M. rubra*

1. **Morus alba** L. (White Mulberry). Shrubby tree to 10 m tall; young branches pubescent. Leaves lobed or unlobed. Flowers in spikes 0.5-2 cm long. Fruit white, pink or blackish purple, 1-2 cm long, edible. Disturbed sites. Middle Florida to Texas and New York. Native of Eurasia; escaped from cultivation. Spring–summer. *Morus nigra* L. (Fig. 21)

2. **Morus rubra** L. (Red Mulberry). Tree to 18 m tall, 3-4 dm in diameter; crown dense, spreading, rounded. Leaves entire, mitten-shaped or 3- to 5-lobed, 8-13 cm long, 5-10 cm wide, scabrous and dull above, moderately pubescent below. Pistillate spikes 1-3 cm long; staminate 4 cm long; fruit dull red, 1.5-3 cm long, edible. Hammocks, pinelands, and thickets. Throughout Florida to Texas, Vermont, and the Dakotas. Spring–summer.

OLACACEAE (Tallowwood Family)

Trees, shrubs, or climbing plants. Leaves alternate, simple. Flow-

Descriptive Flora 57

Fig. 20. *Maclura pomifera* (Osage Orange), × 7/10.

Fig. 21. *Morus alba* (White Mulberry), × 3/5.

ers small, usually bisexual; calyx lobes imbricate; petals 4 to 6, free or partially united; stamens 4 to 12; ovary superior or slightly inferior. Fruit a drupe or nut. About 25 genera, 250 species. Tropics and subtropics.

1. Stem without spines; corolla reddish; fruit nearly enclosed
 by a disk ....1. *Schoepfia*
1. Stems with spines; corolla yellowish; fruit not enclosed
 by a disk ....2. *Ximenia*

1. SCHOEPFIA (Whitewood)

Smooth tree or shrub; bark pale; parasitic on roots of various trees. Leaves entire, alternate. Inflorescence a short raceme, axillary; calyx small; petals 3 to 6, fused into a campanulate corolla. Fruit a drupe. About 38 species. Tropics.

1. **Schoepfia chrysophylloides** (A. Rich.) Planch. (Graytwig). Characters of genus. Coastal hammocks. Rare in central Florida. Tropical Florida to West Indies, Central and South America. All year. (Fig. 22)

Fig. 22. *Schoepfia chrysophylloides* (Graytwig), × 1/2.

2. XIMENIA (Tallowwood)

Small tree or shrub with sharp axillary spines; parasitic on roots of various plants. Leaves entire, elliptic to ovate, mucronate or acuminate at apex. Inflorescence umbellate; calyx minute; petals 4 to 5, distinct, yellowish with reddish pubescence within. Fruit an ellipsoid drupe. About 8 species. Pantropical.

1. **Ximenia americana** L. (Tallowwood). Characters of genus. Wet to dry habitats, hammocks, and scrub. Nearly throughout central Florida to West Indies. All year. (Fig. 23)

Fig. 23. *Ximenia americana* (Tallowwood), × 2/5.

Tallowwood yields a good wood, which is yellow, fine-grained, hard, scented. The fruit is edible, sweetish, and pleasantly flavored.

POLYGONACEAE (Buckwheat Family)

Herbs, shrubs, vines, or trees. Leaves alternate, simple; base of the petiole expanded into a characteristic membranous sheath (ocrea); nodes often swollen. Flowers bisexual or unisexual, small, radial; inflorescence racemose; sepals 3 to 6, becoming membranous in fruit; petals absent; ovary superior; styles 2 to 4. Fruit a 2- to 3-sided nut. About 40 genera, 800 species. Cosmopolitan, but chiefly north temperate.

1. COCCOLOBA (Sea Grape)

Trees or shrubs. Leaves evergreen, entire; ocreae cylindrical, conspicuous. Flowers bisexual or unisexual, usually in spikelike terminal or axillary racemes; perianth 5-parted, becoming fleshy and enclosing the fruit; stamens 8; styles 3. Achene 3-angled, surrounded by fleshy hypanthium. 150 species. Tropical and subtropical America.

1. Leaves orbicular, broader than long, cordate at base, thick .2. *C. uvifera*
1. Leaves lance-ovate, longer than broad, tapering to base, thin ....1. *C. diversifolia*

1. **Coccoloba diversifolia** Jacq. (Pigeon Plum). Trees or shrubs. Leaves 6-10 cm long, cuneate or rounded at base. Flowers in racemes, 5-8 cm long; perianth parts up to 3.5 mm long. Fruit black, in drooping clusters. Hammocks. Rare in central Florida. South Florida to West Indies, Central and South America. Spring–fall. *Coccolobis laurifolia* Jacq.

2. **Coccoloba uvifera** (L.) L. (Sea Grape). Small tree to 5 m tall; twigs contorted and fluted. Leaves suborbicular to 20 cm wide, cordate; reddish on drying. Flowers in racemes on a pendulous rachis over 2 dm long. Fruits 3-angled, purple. Coastal hammocks and dunes. Florida to West Indies, Central and South America. Spring–fall. (Fig. 24)

The wood is close-grained, hard, and may be used in the cabinet industry. The tree is often planted as an ornamental.

NYCTAGINACEAE (Four O'Clock Family)

Trees or shrubs or herbs. Leaves alternate or opposite. Flowers bisexual or unisexual; usually cymose with brightly colored bracts that

62 TREES OF CENTRAL FLORIDA

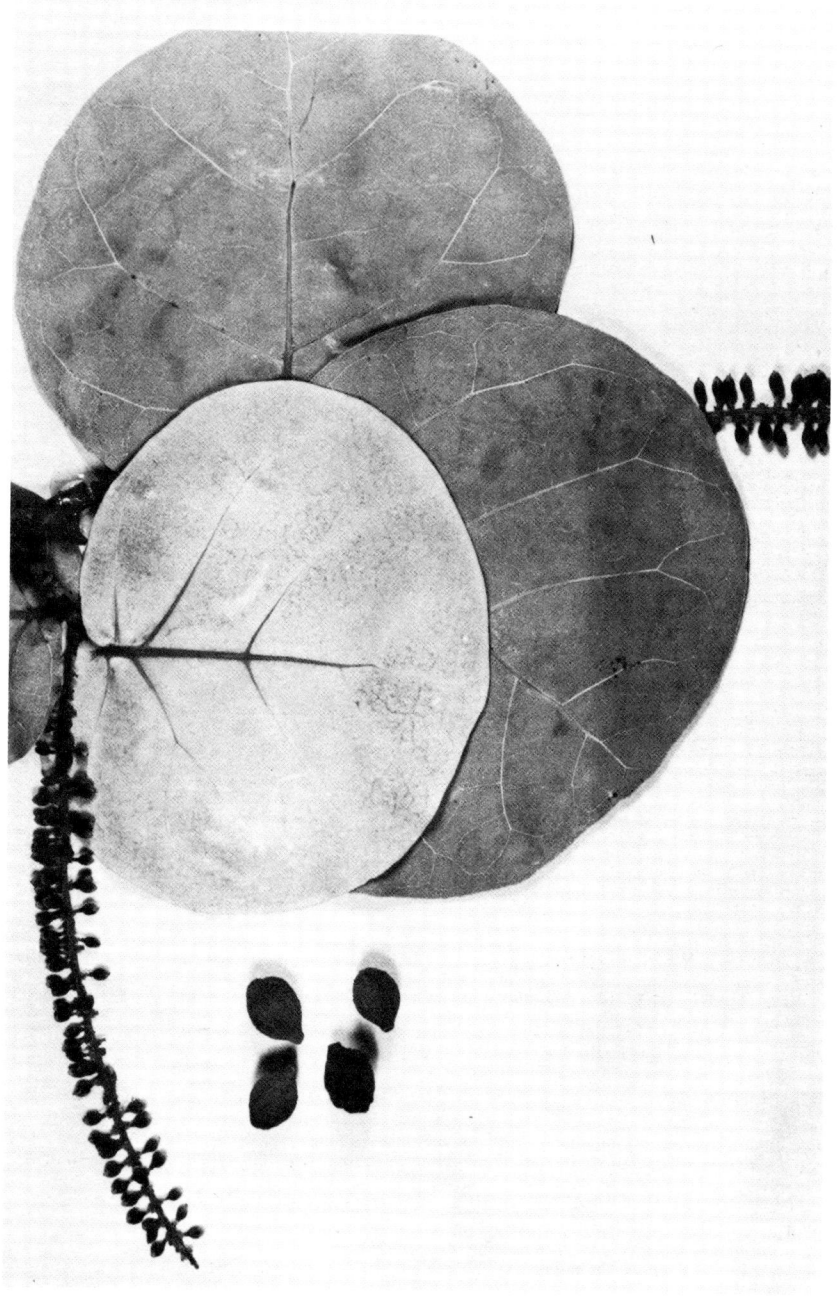

Fig. 24. *Coccoloba uvifera* (Sea Grape), × 3/5.

simulate a calyx; perianth tubular, often petaloid; stamens 1 to many. Fruit indehiscent. About 30 genera, 290 species. Tropics and subtropics, mostly American.

GUAPIRA (Blolly)

Trees, shrubs, or vines, with or without spines. Leaves entire, opposite or alternate. Inflorescence cymose; flowers unisexual, on separate plants, small; corolla absent; pistillate flowers tubular. Fruit glandular or eglandular. About 50 species. Tropics and subtropics.

1. **Guapira discolor** (Spreng.) Little (Blolly). Shrub or small tree with pale, smooth bark and short internodes; without spines. Leaves variable. Flowers greenish yellow, racemose or paniculate. Fruit drupaceous, without glands, scarlet or red, juicy. Coastal hammocks and dune scrub. Atlantic Coast of Florida, south Florida, and West Indies. Spring–fall. *Pisonia discolor* Spreng.; *Pisonia discolor* var. *longifolia* Heimerl; *Torrubia longifolia* (Heimerl) Britt.; *Torrubia globosa* Small; *Torrubia bracei* Britt. (Fig. 25)

MAGNOLIACEAE (Magnolia Family)

Tree, trunk straight, tapering; crown pyramidal; branches ascending. Leaves evergreen or deciduous, elliptic or oblong, cuneate at base; stipules connate, hooded over leaf buds, falling as leaf unfolds. Flowers bisexual, solitary, large, fragrant; sepals and petals in cycles of 3; stamens and pistils numerous, spirally imbricate. Fruit an aggregation of follicles. About 12 genera, 230 species. Temperate and tropical regions.

1. Leaves 4- to 6-lobed, truncate or broadly notched at apex 1. *Liriodendron*
1. Leaves not lobed, rounded to acute at apex ....2. *Magnolia*

1. LIRIODENDRON (Tulip Tree)

Trees to 60 m tall. Leaves deciduous; blades lobed, truncate or broadly notched at apex. Flowers greenish yellow with orange blotches at center, cup-shaped, solitary; petals 6; sepals 3, reflexed. Fruit a cone of appressed samaralike carpels. 2 species. Eastern United States and China.

1. **Liriodendron tulipifera** L. (Tulip Tree). Characters of genus. Wet woods. Orange County northward to Arkansas, Michigan, Massachusetts. Summer. (Fig. 26)

Fig. 25. *Gaupira discolor* (Blolly), × 4/5.

2. MAGNOLIA (Magnolia)

Trees or shrubs. Leaves evergreen or deciduous, often large, entire; stipules free or fused to petiole. Flowers at first enclosed by 1 to several bracts, often erect, white; sepals and petals about equal in length. Fruit in conelike clusters, carpels dehisce longitudinally. About 80 species. Southeast Asia and America.

1. Leaves rusty tomentose to glabrous below; petals over 5 cm long; fruit cones 8-12 cm long; carpels numerous . . . . 1. *M. grandiflora*
1. Leaves glaucous below; petals less than 5 cm long; fruit cones 3-5 cm long; carpels few . . . . 2. *M. virginiana*

Fig. 26. *Liriodendron tulipifera* (Tulip Tree), × 4/5.

1. **Magnolia grandiflora** L. (Southern Magnolia). Tree to 25 m tall. Leaf evergreen, blades 10-20 cm long, 5-10 cm wide, thick, leathery, lustrous green above, persistently rusty pubescent below or glaucous; petioles stout. Flowers creamy white, very fragrant, 15-20 cm across; petals 6 to 12, variable in size and shape; perianth and stamens soon deciduous; velvety spathe covering both leaf and flower buds. Fruit woody, conelike, to 10 cm long; seeds bright, lustrous red. Wet to mesic woods. Middle Florida to Texas and North Carolina. Spring–summer.

Southern magnolia is one of the most strikingly beautiful of the native trees of Florida. The skyward reach of the tree is portrayed by the erect, tapering trunk through the crown and the vertically oriented leaf and flower buds. The hooded stipules on elongation become white, like candles set on the twigs. The great beauty of the tree culminates in scented flowers that open skyward. The 9 to 12 white petals in whorls of 3, spread bowl-fashion, sometimes to 20 cm wide, and the blades are narrowed to claws forming portals for bees around the floral axis that subtends the numerous stamens and pistils. The stigmas of the pistil cover the dome-shaped apex of the axis and recurve in full expansion. Below, a band of whitish yellow anthers readily fall, after ripening and pollination. Maturing seeds in the ovaries assure continuity of life as the parts develop into upright, multiple, reddish, conelike fruits. Each follicle on opening discloses usually 2, scarlet, suspended, ripe, lustrous seeds.

2. **Magnolia virginiana** L. (Sweet Bay). Tree to 6-10 m tall, 2-4 dm in diameter; bark smooth, pale gray; young twigs green, white pubescent, later smooth. Leaves evergreen, alternate, simple, thin-leathery, green and shiny above, smooth and silvery beneath. Flowers about 5 cm wide, fragrant, symmetrically urn-shaped at first, spreading later; petals 9 to 12. Fruiting cones ellipsoid, 3-5 cm long; seeds red, glabrous. Wet woods and margins of swamps. Throughout Florida to Texas and Massachusetts. Spring–fall. (Fig. 27)

ILLICIACEAE (Anise Tree Family)

Shrubs or small trees, aromatic. Leaves evergreen, 6-15 cm long, exstipulate, elliptic, alternate or clustered at ends of twigs. Flowers solitary or 2 to 3 together, axillary or subterminal, appearing crowded among leaves at tips of branchlets. Perianth segments many in series of 3 or more; stamens numerous, in series, erect, with fleshy filaments. Fruit a whorl of free-spreading follicles 10-18 mm long, dehiscing along the upper side. 1 genus, 42 species. Asia, Malaysia, North America, Mexico, and West Indies.

1. ILLICIUM (Anise Tree)

Characters of the family. 42 species. Asia, Malaysia, North America, Mexico, and West Indies.

1. **Illicium parviflorum** Michx. ex Vent. (Star Anise). Characters of the family. Low woods and swamps. Northeastern counties of our area to Georgia. Spring. (Fig. 28)

Fig. 27. *Magnolia virginiana* (Sweet Bay), × 3/5.

ANNONACEAE (Custard Apple Family)

Trees, shrubs, or climbing plants. Leaves simple, alternate, tardily deciduous or evergreen. Flowers bisexual, solitary in axils; sepals and petals in cycles of 3; stamens free; receptacle convex, terminating with numerous simple pistils above the stamens. Fruiting carpels free, often a fleshy berry, or united into an aggregate fruit. 120 genera, 2100 species. Chiefly Old World but few in American tropics.

1. Carpels numerous and confluent, forming an aggregate fruit .1. *Annona*
1. Carpels few and distinct, forming a simple fruit . . . . .2. *Asimina*

1. ANNONA (Custard Apple)

Trees or shrubs. Leaves evergreen, thick, pinnately veined. Flowers solitary or in few-flowered clusters; sepals 3; stamens many. Fruit

68 TREES OF CENTRAL FLORIDA

Fig. 28. *Illicium parviflorum* (Star Anise), × 1/2.

aggregated and coalescent on the receptacle. 110 species. Chiefly tropical America.

1. Petals more than 1 cm wide, fruit smooth ....1. *A. glabra*
1. Petals less than 1 cm wide, fruit tuberculate ....2. *A. squamosa*

1. **Annona glabra** L. (Pond Apple). Tree to 10 m tall, buttressed at base; trunk tapering to densely branched; rounded crown; twigs reddish, glandular, reticulated. Leaves 7-14 cm long, elliptic-lanceolate to oblong, pale green, usually acute at apex. Flowers solitary from about the middle of the internodes below the leaves on often drooping pedicels, 1-2 cm long; sepals uniform or rounded, about 4-5 mm long; outer petals white, 2.5-3 mm long. Fruit globose, smooth, 7-12 cm long, yellow blotched with brown. Mangrove swamps and freshwater swamps. Brevard County to tropical America. Spring. (Fig. 29)

2. **Annona squamosa** L. (Sugar Apple). Shrubs or small trees to 10 m tall; branches smooth. Leaves mostly 10-15 mm long, lance-elliptic to elliptic-ovate, acute or sometimes obtuse at apex. Flowers solitary; sepals deltoid-acute, about 2 mm long; outer petals 2.5-3 cm long. Fruit 6-10 cm long, ellipsoid to subglobose, yellowish green, tuberculate. Hammocks. Lee County. Native of tropical America. Summer.

2. ASIMINA (Pawpaw)

Shrubs or trees. Leaves deciduous or evergreen, alternate, with pungent odor when bruised. Flowers axillary, solitary or in small clusters; short-pedicelled, nodding; sepals 3, soon deciduous; petals 6, the inner small, erect; pistils 3 to 15, but only a few maturing. Fruit 1 to few, oval or oblong, fleshy berries. 10 species. Eastern United States.

1. **Asimina parviflora** (Michx.) Dunal. (Dwarf Pawpaw). Small tree or shrub. Leaf blades obovate, elliptic-obovate or cuneate-obovate, 6-17 cm long, acuminate or acute. Flowers maroon; pedicels 5 mm long or less, tomentose; sepals broadly ovate; outer petals ovate or nearly so, 7-10 mm long, densely pubescent; saccate bases of inner petals never corrugate. Fruit ovoid or ellipsoid, berries 2-6 cm long. Rich woods and hammocks. Middle Florida to Mississippi and North Carolina. Spring. (Fig. 30)

LAURACEAE (Laurel Family)

Trees or shrubs or vines. Leaves aromatic, alternate, simple. Flowers small, bisexual, or if unisexual on same or different plants,

Fig. 29. *Annona glabra* (Pond Apple), × 1/2.

apetalous, numerous; inflorescence axillary or terminal raceme or cyme; calyx 4- to 6-lobed; stamens 12 in 3 or 4 whorls; ovary superior. Fruit a berry or drupe. About 35 genera, 2500 species. Tropics and warm temperate areas of both hemispheres.

1. Leaves with glands in the axils of the basal veins on lower surface ....1. *Cinnamomum*
1. Leaves without glands in the axils of the basal veins on lower surface 2

Descriptive Flora 71

Fig. 30. *Asimina parviflora* (Dwarf Pawpaw), × 1/2.

2. Leaves deciduous, heteromorphic .... 4. *Sassafras*
2. Leaves evergreen, not heteromorphic 3
3. Staminodes small, filamentous .... 2. *Nectandra*
3. Staminodes large, broad .... 3. *Persea*

1. CINNAMOMUM (Cinnamon)

Shrubs and trees. Leaves evergreen with camphor odor, alternate (or opposite). Inflorescences paniculate, axillary, with deciduous bracts; flowers inconspicuous, bisexual; calyx short with 6 segments, subequal; stamens usually 5 to 9 in 3 series, fourth series of staminodes. Fruit a black, globose drupe. 100 to 275 species. Eastern Asia.

1. **Cinnamomum camphora** (L.) Nees & Eberm. (Camphor Tree). Character of genus. Pinelands and thickets. Scattered localities from Florida to Georgia, Louisiana and Texas, and in California. Native of Asia, escaped from cultivation. Spring. *Camphora camphora* (L.) Karst. (Fig. 31)

Fig. 31. *Cinnamomum camphora* (Camphor Tree), × 1/2.

Camphor is obtained by the distillation of wood of this species. The tree was introduced into Florida in 1875 and later established in plantations in an attempt to promote a camphor industry in Florida to compete with that of Formosa and Japan. The venture was not profitable. At present, the camphor tree is cultivated in central Florida as an ornamental and for windbreaks. It is hardy to 15 degrees Fahrenheit.

2. NECTANDRA (Lancewood)

Trees or shrubs to 13 m tall. Leaves evergreen, alternate or subopposite, entire. Flowers bisexual, pedicelled, in axillary or subterminal panicles; sepals 6, equal, often reflexed; outer series of stamens petaloid and fleshy; style short; stigmas capitate. Fruit a drupe, ellipsoid or subglobose, with a shallow, woody cupule. About 175 species. Tropical America.

1. **Nectandra coriacea** (Sw.) Griseb. (Lancewood). Characters of the genus. Coastal hammocks. Volusia County southward to West Indies. All year. (Fig. 32)

3. PERSEA (Bay Tree)

Trees or tall shrubs. Leaves evergreen, alternate. Flowers yellowish, in small axillary or terminal panicles; calyx campanulate, 6-lobed; stamens in 3 series, often all fertile. Fruit globose or pyriform. About 150 species. Tropics and subtropics.

1. Calyx deciduous; fruit over 5 cm long . . . . 1. *P. americana*
1. Calyx persistent; fruit less than 3 cm long 2
    2. Under surface of leaves, petioles, buds white pubescent to nearly glabrous . . . . 2. *P. borbonia*
    2. Under surface of leaves, petioles, buds rusty-tomentose or sericeous 3
3. Pubescence dull, rusty-tomentose .4. *P. palustris*
3. Pubescence lustrous, sericeous . . . . .3. *P. humilis*

1. **Persea americana** Mill. (Avocado). Tree up to 20 m tall. Leaves about 10-30 cm long, elliptic or obovate-oblong, coriaceous, dark green. Flowers about 6-7 mm long, in axillary panicles; sepals yellow green, deciduous; ovary pubescent. Fruit large, pyriform, 7-20 cm long, the pulp fleshy, oily. Hammocks and low, moist areas. Scattered localities in our area. Native of tropical America, escaped from cultivation. Spring. *Persea persea* (L.) Cockerell

The avocado was introduced into Florida by the Spaniards. It has become an important crop in southern Florida with plantations extending north to Brevard and Hillsborough counties.

Fig. 32. *Nectandra coriacea* (Lancewood), × 1/2.

2. **Persea borbonia** (L.) Spreng. (Redbay). Shrub or tree up to 20 m tall; young stems thinly pubescent or glabrous; bark coppery brown, aromatic. Leaves 3-13 cm long, elliptic, rigid, bright green above, coppery sheen below, mostly glabrous. Flowers about 5 mm long, silky without, glabrous within; peduncles tomentose. Fruits blue black, about 1 cm long. Hammocks, dunes, and low woods. Throughout Florida to Texas and North Carolina. Spring–fall. *Tamala borbonia* (L.) Raf.; *Tamala littoralis* Small (Fig. 33)

3. **Persea humilis** Nash (Silk Bay). Small tree. Leaves with shining golden hairs beneath, glabrous above, elliptic, 4-10 cm long, more or less revolute. Inflorescence reduced; sepals erect, obtuse, 5 mm long. Fruit a globular drupe about 1.5 cm long, purplish black under the bloom. White sand scrub. Central counties of Florida. Spring. *Tamala humilis* (Nash) Small; *Persea borbonia* var. *humilis* (Nash) Kopp

4. **Persea palustris** (Raf.) Sarg. (Swamp Bay). Shrub or tree up to 15 m tall; young branches densely rusty tomentose. Leaves 10-15 cm long, lanceolate to oblong, thinly pubescent becoming glabrate beneath; petiole 1-2 cm long, tomentose. Inflorescence a many-flowered panicle with tomentose peduncles. Fruit subglobose, 10-18 mm wide. Wet soil and swamps. Florida to Texas and Virginia. Spring. *Tamala pubescens* (Pursh) Small

4. SASSAFRAS (Sassafras)

Shrubs or trees up to 15 m tall, aromatic; bark dark reddish brown, smooth or shallowly furrowed at the base of the trunk; crown open, flattish. Leaves deciduous, often lobed, palmately veined. Flowers greenish yellow, unisexual, on different plants; in loose peduncled clusters at ends of branches; calyx accrescent and persistent. Fruit a blue drupe about 1 cm long. 3 species. China and North America.

1. **Sassafras albidum** (Nutt.) Nees (Sassafras). Characters of genus. Woods and fields. Hillsborough County and from Orange County northward to Texas, Michigan, and Massachusetts. Spring. *Sassafras sassafras* (L.) Karst. (Fig. 34)

Oil of sassafras distilled from root bark is used in soaps, perfumes, and ointments. The bark of the roots is processed by drying and is marketed as sassafras tea.

CAPPARACEAE (Caper Family)

Trees, shrubs, vines, or herbs. Leaves alternate, simple or digitately compound. Flowers bisexual, in racemes or cymes, or solitary;

Fig. 33. *Persea borbonia* (Redbay), × 2/5.

Fig. 34. *Sassafras albidum* (Sassafras), × 1/2.

sepals 4 or 5; petals 4; stamens few to many. Fruit capsular, berrylike. 30 genera, 650 species. Tropical and warm temperate regions.

1. CAPPARIS (Caper)

Trees or shrubs; branches lepidote to glabrate. Leaves simple, entire. Sepals 4, free or fused at the base; petals 4; stamens numerous; ovary long-stipitate; style wanting. Fruit a fleshy capsule. 250 species. Pantropical.

1. Upper stems and lower surface of leaves lepidote 1. *C. cynophallophora*
1. Upper stems and lower surface of leaves glabrous . . . . . . .2. *C. flexuosa*

1. **Capparis cynophallophora** L. (Jamaica Caper). Shrub or small tree to 6 m tall; branches densely lepidote to glabrate. Leaves 5-20 cm long, elliptic to obovate, leathery, densely lepidote beneath. Flowers white to purplish or brownish in corymbose, terminal or axillary inflorescences; sepals 7-12 mm long; petals ovate, 8-16 mm long. Fruit body elongating to 15-40 cm long. Coastal hammocks and shell mounds. Brevard and Pinellas counties, southward to West Indies and Mexico. Spring–summer.

2. **Capparis flexuosa** L. (Limber Caper). Shrub or small tree to 8 m tall; branches glabrous. Leaves 4-16 cm long, varying from linear to broadly obovate, glabrate. Flowers white or pale pink, few, corymbose-paniculate, terminal; sepals 7-10 mm long; petals 1-15 cm long, glabrous. Fruit an irregular, fleshy capsule up to 15 cm long with a basal stipe 1-9 cm long. Coastal hammocks and shell mounds. Brevard County southward along east coast to South Florida, West Indies, and South America. Spring–summer. (Fig. 35)

HAMAMELIDACEAE (Witch-Hazel Family)

Trees or shrubs. Leaves alternate, deciduous or evergreen, simple, toothed to palmately lobed, stipulate. Flowers axillary in spikes or heads, bisexual or unisexual, radially symmetrical or sometimes bilaterally; sepals 4 or 5; petals 4 or 5 or perianth absent; stamens 2 to 8; ovary half-inferior to inferior, 2 locular; styles and stigmas 2. Fruit a capsule. About 23 genera, 100 species. Widely distributed.

1. Leaves pinnately veined . . . . .1. *Hamamelis*
1. Leaves palmately lobed and veined . . . . .2. *Liquidambar*

1. HAMAMELIS (Witch-hazel)

Shrub or rarely small tree. Leaves straight-veined, deciduous,

Fig. 35. *Capparis flexuosa* (Limber Caper), × 1/2.

short-petioled, obovate to oval or suborbicular. Flowers bisexual, in small axillary, pedunculate clusters, usually surrounded by scalelike, 3-parted involucre; calyx 4-parted with 2 or 3 bractlets at its base; petals 4; stamens 4, very short, opposite petals. Fruit a bivalved capsule; seed 1 in each cell, black lustrous. 6 species. North America and Asia.

    1. **Hamamelis virginiana** L. (Witch-hazel). Characters of genus.

Low woods and moist hillsides. Lake County, northward to Texas, Minnesota, and New York. Fall. (Fig. 36)

The bark is used medicinally.

Fig. 36. *Hamamelis virginiana* (Witch-Hazel), × 2/5.

2. LIQUIDAMBAR (Sweet Gum)

Tree up to 25 m tall. Leaves palmately lobed. Flowers in globular heads or aments; stamens in conical clusters, numerous, intermixed with small scales; pistillate inflorescence with numerous 2-beaked, 2-locular ovaries, cohering and becoming hard in fruit, forming a spherical ament. Seeds with wing-angled seed coat. 4 species. Asia and North America.

1. **Liquidambar styraciflua** L. (Sweet Gum). Characters of genus. Tree usually with corky ridges on branchlets. Leaves turn brilliant red in autumn. Moist to wet deciduous woods. Nearly throughout the range of this manual to Texas and Missouri. Spring. (Fig. 37)

A fragrant balsam is obtained from all species of sweet gum. The wood is known as satin walnut.

Fig. 37. *Liquidambar styraciflua* (Sweet Gum), × 2/5.

ROSACEAE (Rose Family)

Trees, shrubs, or herbs. Leaves alternate, simple or compound, often stipulate. Flowers usually bisexual, radially symmetrical, 5-merous; calyx free or fused to ovary; corolla generally free; stamens numerous; ovary superior or inferior; styles free. Fruits variable — drupes, pomes, hips, achenes, or aggregations. About 100 genera, 3000 species. Cosmopolitan.

1. Ovary inferior, adnate to calyx or hypanthium;
   fruit a pome .... 1. *Crataegus*
1. Ovary superior, united to calyx tube only at the base;
   fruit a drupe .... 2. *Prunus*

1. CRATAEGUS (Hawthorn)

Trees or shrubs with ascending to spreading branches; twigs spiny. Leaves simple, serrate or lobed, stipules foliose, deciduous. Flowers borne in simple or compound corymbs or cymes; ovary inferior with 1 to 5 carpels; petals 5; stamens 5 to 25; styles 1 to 5, distinct. Fruit a red, yellow, or orange pome, subglobose or pyriform, 1 to 5 nutlets imbedded in the flesh. About 200 species. North temperate regions.

1. Leaf margins without glands 2
1. Leaf margins with glands .... 1. *C. flava*
   2. Leaf base truncate or nearly so; leaf blade deeply
      3- to 7-lobed .... 2. *C. marshallii*
   2. Leaf base cuneate or attenuate; leaf blade usually only
      slightly lobed .... 3. *C. viridis*

1. Crataegus flava Ait. (Summer Haw). Tree to 6 m tall with spines 5-6 cm long; young branches woolly. Leaves with black gland-tipped teeth, rounded or pointed at apex, base cuneate, pubescent. Flowers in simple cymes, 3- to 5-flowered, pedicels pubescent, 3-5 mm long; sepals lanceolate, 3-6 cm long; stamens 15 to 20. Fruit red, globose, 8-17 mm in diameter. Woodlands. Middle Florida northward to Alabama, Tennessee, and Georgia. Spring. *Crataegus michauxii* Pers.; *Crataegus floridana* Sarg.

2. Crataegus marshallii (Parsley Haw). Slender tree to 6 m tall; crown narrow; branches slender, often contorted; thorny; bark grayish brown, exfoliating in thin plates. Leaves deltoid-ovate, blades and petioles each about 4 cm long. Flowers 15 mm wide, in corymbose cymes; petals white; stamens 10, filaments pink. Fruit red, ellipsoid,

5-7 mm long; nutlets 1 to 3. Moist woods. Hillsborough County northward to Texas and Virginia. Spring. (Fig. 38)

3. **Crataegus viridis** L. (Green Haw). Tree to 10 m tall; branches wide spreading, slender; branchlets sometimes thorny; bark gray or reddish brown. Leaves ovate, oblong-ovate or elliptic, usually more or less lobed, glabrous. Flowers 1.2-1.5 cm wide, mostly 8 to 20 in compound corymbs; stamens 20. Fruit subglobose, 5-8 mm long, bright-red or orange; nutlets 4 or 5. Stream margins. Rare in central Florida, Marion County only. Northern Florida to Texas, Kansas. Spring.

PRUNUS (Plum, Cherry)

Small or medium-sized trees; bark astringent, exudes a gummy substance, conspicuous transverse lenticels present, peels away in papery, horizontal plates. Leaves alternate, simple, stipulate, deciduous or evergreen. Flowers borne in umbels, or solitary from axillary shoots, or in terminal or axillary racemes; sepals 5, sometimes glandular, alternating with 5 petals around the rim of the cuplike hypanthium; 5 to 30 stamens within; pistil simple; style 1; stigma capitate; ovary superior. Fruit a drupe. 430 species. North temperate.

1. Flowers in racemes 2
1. Flowers solitary or in clusters 3
    2. Racemes terminal on present season's growth,
        over 4 cm long . . . . .4. *P. serotina*
    2. Racemes axillary on previous season's growth,
        less than 4 cm long . . . . .3. *P. caroliniana*
3. Margins of sepal lobes ciliate, not glandular; serrations of
    leaves sometimes gland-tipped .2. *P. angustifolia*
3. Margins of sepal lobes not ciliate, glandular; serrations of
    leaves lacking glands . . . . .1. *P. americana*

1. **Prunus americana** Marsh. (Wild Plum). Tree up to 10 m with spreading branches, sometimes thorny; bark tan, becomes shaggy. Leaves elliptic-obovate or obovate, 7-10.5 cm long, pubescent at least beneath, rounded to subcordate at base, apices short-acuminate. Flowers about 2.5 cm wide, white, borne in umbels of 2 (5), fragrant. Fruit a subglobose drupe, 2.5 cm long, bluish or purplish. Edges of woods, along fences, and streams. Highlands and DeSoto counties northward to Colorado, Montana, and New York. Spring.

2. **Prunus angustifolia** Marsh. (Chickasaw Plum). Tree to 6 m tall or much-branched shrub forming thickets. Leaves deciduous, bright

Fig. 38. *Crataegus marshallii* (Parsley Haw), × 4/5.

green above, paler below, 3-6 cm long, conspicuously folded lengthwise, lanceolate, finely serrate, teeth incurved. Flowers in clusters of 2 to 4, opening before leaf expansion; petals 4-6 mm long, white. Fruit subglobose, 12-20 mm in diameter, red to yellow. Edges of woods and along fences. DeSoto County, northward to Texas, Kansas, and New Jersey. Spring.

3. **Prunus caroliniana** Ait. (Carolina Laurel Cherry). Tree to 10 m tall; crown cylindrical of spreading, ascending branches; bark rough with interlacing furrows. Leaves evergreen, dark green above, paler below, 3-12 cm long, acuminate, rounded bases, margins entire or sparsely sharp-toothed. Flowers white, in dense axillary racemes; sepals minute; petals angulate. Fruit a drupe, 10-13 mm long; stone ovoid. Hammocks, thickets, and along streams. DeSoto County northward to Texas and North Carolina. Spring. *Laurocerasus caroliniana* (Mill.) Roem. (Fig 39)

The tree may be used as a windbreak or trimmed for hedges. The fruit furnishes food for birds. The leaves contain prussic acid and are poisonous to livestock.

4. **Prunus serotina** Ehrh. (Wild Cherry). Tree to 20 m tall; crown cylindrical, open; bark reddish brown, lenticels numerous, horizontal. Leaves 5-15 cm long, midvein hairy at base below, blades oblong-ovate with long pointed tips, bright green. Flowers in racemes, 6-14 cm long; calyx persistent; corolla 8-10 mm broad. Fruit a globose drupe, purple, juicy, edible; stone prominently ridged. Woods and roadsides. Northwestern counties in central Florida, north to Texas and North Dakota. Spring. *Padus virginiana* (L.) Mill.

The wilted foliage is dangerously poisonous to animals. Formerly the wood was used in cabinetwork but currently large trees are scarce.

CHRYSOBALANACEAE (Coco-plum Family)

Trees or shrubs. Leaves alternate, simple, entire. Flowers bisexual, rarely unisexual, borne in panicles; calyx 5-parted, corolla of 5 petals, often unequal, inserted in mouth of calyx tube; stamens 2 to many, filiform. Fruit a drupe. 10 genera, 400 species. Tropics and subtropics.

1. CHRYSOBALANUS (Cocoplum)

Small trees or shrubs. Leaves evergreen, leathery, variable in shape, 2-8 cm long. Flowers small, white, in axillary cymes; petals 5

Fig. 39. *Prunus caroliniana* (Carolina Laurel Cherry), × 1/2.

and clawed; stamens 15 or more. Fruit a drupe, subglobose, 2-5 cm long, white to purple. 4 species. Tropical Africa and America.

    1. **Chrysobalanus icaco** L. (Cocoplum). Characters of genus. Coastal area and hammocks. Coastal counties from Brevard southward to South Florida, West Indies, and tropical America. All year. *Chrysobalanus interior* Small; *Chrysobalanus icaco* var. *pellocarpus* (Meyer) DC. (Fig. 40)

Fig. 40. *Chrysobalanus icaco* (Cocoplum), × 1/2.

FABACEAE (Pea Family)

Herbs, shrubs, vines, or trees. Leaves alternate, pinnate, bipinnate, 1-foliate or simple. Flowers usually in terminal racemes, panicles, spikes or heads, occasionally in umbels or cymes or solitary, bisexual, irregular or regular; calyx 5-parted; petals 5 or reduced to 1; stamens 10 or fewer or numerous, distinct, monodelphous, or diadelphous; pistil 1, simple; ovary superior. Fruit a dehiscent or indehiscent legume. 600 genera, 12,000 species. Cosmopolitan.

1. Leaves simple 2
1. Leaves pinnately compound 3
   2. Leaves cordate; flowers pseudopapilionaceous ....5. *Cercis*
   2. Leaves bilobed at apex; flowers not
      pseudopapilionaceous ....3. *Bauhinia*
3. Plants armed with spines 4
3. Plants unarmed 7
   4. Flowers radially symmetrical 5
   4. Flowers bilaterally symmetrical 6
5. Leaves with 2 pinnae, each reduced to 1 pair of leaflets;
   legume contorted; seeds arillate ....12. *Pithecellobium*
5. Leaves with 2 to 6 pinnae, each with 10 to 20 pairs of leaflets;
   legume turgid; seeds not arillate ....1. *Acacia*
   6. Leaf rachis phyllodial; leaflets much reduced;
      spines short, simple ....10. *Parkinsonia*
   6. Leaf rachis not phyllodial; leaflets not much reduced;
      spines long, often branched ....8. *Gleditsia*
7. Leaves once compound 8
7. Leaves twice compound 10
   8. Leaves odd-pinnate ....11. *Piscidia*
   8. Leaves even-pinnate 9
9. Leaflets 3 or 4 pairs ....4. *Cassia*
9. Leaflets 9 to 14 pairs ....13. *Tamarindus*
   10. Flowers radially symmetrical, in capitate clusters, cream or
      pale yellow; fruits with thin or short, woody, coiled valves 11
   10. Flowers bilaterally symmetrical, in panicles, bright red;
      fruits with long, woody, straight valves ....6. *Delonix*
11. Fruits straight, valves thin 12
11. Fruits coiled, valves woody ....7. *Enterolobium*
   12. Leaflets 2-3 mm wide ....9. *Leucaena*
   12. Leaflets 8-20 mm wide ....2. *Albizia*

1. ACACIA (Acacia)

Trees or shrubs usually armed with stipular spines. Leaves bipinnate. Flowers in spikes or racemes subtended by axillary peduncles, bisexual; calyx and corolla 4- to 6-cleft; stamens numerous, filaments free or slightly united. Legume cylindrical, compressed, dry or pulpy within. About 800 species. Tropics and subtropics.

1. **Acacia farnesiana** (L.) Willd. (Sweet Acacia). Leaves with 2 to 6 pairs of pinnae; leaflets 10 to 20 pairs per pinna. Flower spikes dense, globose, yellow. Fruit turgid. Hammocks, dry pinelands, and coastal strand. Various coastal counties. South Florida to Louisiana, Mexico, and West Indies. Spring. *Vachellia farnesiana* (L.) Wright & Arn. (Fig. 41)

2. ALBIZIA

Trees, unarmed. Leaves deciduous, even-pinnate; leaflets numerous; petiolar gland next to axil at base. Inflorescence paniculate; flowers bisexual or polygamous; calyx of united sepals; corolla funnelform; stamens numerous, long-exserted, filaments united below middle. Legume linear, flat. 100 to 150 species. Old World tropics and subtropics.

1. **Albizia lebbeck** (L.) Benth. (Woman's Tongue). Leaves 20-35 mm long, 4- to 8-pinnate; leaflets 10 to 22, blades oblique, broadly obtuse. Flowers in pedunculate, globose heads, cream colored; stamens to 3 mm long, filaments bright yellow. Legume to 20 cm long, 7- to 10-seeded. Hammocks. Central Florida. Native of Old World. Escaped from cultivation. Florida and West Indies. Spring. (Fig. 42)

3. BAUHINIA (Orchid Tree)

Trees or shrubs. Leaves broad, entire or 2-cleft or lobed. Flowers yellow, white, rose, or red, in simple or panicled terminal or axillary racemes; calyx variously lobed or cleft, in some species opening on one side and remaining as a single spathelike organ; petals 5, somewhat unequal, usually narrowed into a claw; stamens 10, or reduced to 5 or 1. Fruit a long, flat legume, dehiscent or indehiscent. 250 to 300 species. Pantropical.

1. **Bauhinia variegata** L. (Orchid Tree). Tree, medium size, unarmed. Leaves 5-10 cm long, thick, nearly truncate or cordate at base, apex 2-lobed one-third the length of blade, lobes obtuse. Flowers few, axillary, showy and fragrant, 7.5-10 cm wide, lavender to purple, vexillum mottled with purple; calyx tube 2-5 cm long, equalling or exceeding the limb; petals obovate, narrowed to a claw; fertile stamens 5 or 6. Legume up to 30 cm long, flat, sharp-beaked, stipitate. Shell mounds and disturbed areas. Brevard and Lee counties and probably

Fig. 41. *Acacia farnesiana* (Sweet Acacia), × 3/4.

Fig. 42. *Albizia lebbeck* (Woman's Tongue), × 1/2.

elsewhere. Florida and West Indies. Native of India. Escaped from cultivation. Spring. (Fig. 43)

4. CASSIA (Senna)

Trees, shrubs, or herbs. Leaves evenly 1-pinnate. Inflorescence axillary or terminal; flowers bisexual; sepals united into a short tube; petals yellow or reddish, often unlike; stamens 10 or fewer by abortion, unequal; ovary sessile or stipitate. Legume dehiscent or indehiscent, 1- to several-seeded. 500 to 600 species. Tropics and warm temperate regions.

1. **Cassia coluteoides** Coll. (Cassia). Small tree or shrub. Leaflets 3 or 4 pair, 1.5-3 cm long, obovate-elliptic, glabrous, punctate on lower surface. Legume turgid, stipitate, 6-15 cm long, curved. Canal banks and mangroves. Brevard and Hendry counties. Florida, West Indies. All year. (Fig. 44)

5. CERCIS (Redbud)

Trees or shrubs. Leaves deciduous, 1-foliate; leaflets broad. Flowers in whorls of 4 to 8, pseudopapilionaceous, rose to bright pink; calyx shallowly lobed, tube gibbous; keel petal of corolla longer than others. Legume thin, flat, persistent. 6 species. North temperate regions.

1. **Cercis canadensis** L. (Redbud). Leaf blades entire, broadly cordate to reniform, 7.5-12.5 cm long. Flowers appear prior to leaves. Legumes to 7.5 cm long. Dry, rich woods. Citrus County northward. Florida to Texas, Nebraska, Ohio, and Connecticut. Winter–spring. (Fig. 45)

Redbud is commonly planted throughout and slightly outside its range.

6. DELONIX (Flamboyant)

Trees or shrubs. Leaves evenly bipinnate; leaflets small, numerous, blades narrow. Flowers showy; 5-merous, sepals shorter than petals, blades of petals flabellate, long-clawed; stamens distinct, long-exserted. Legume elongate, linear, flat. 3 species. Africa and Asia.

1. **Delonix regia** (Boj. ex Hook.) Raf. (Royal Poinciana). Leaves 3-5 dm long with up to 20 pinnae. Sepals red within; petals flame red; standard mottled. Legume up to 6 dm long, compressed, solid between seeds. Hammocks. Lee County. Florida and West Indies. Native of Africa and Madagascar. Escaped from cultivation. Spring–summer. *Poinciana regia* Boj. (Fig. 46)

Fig. 43. *Bauhinia variegata* (Orchid Tree), × 1/2.

Fig. 44. *Cassia coluteoides* (Cassia), × 1/2.

Fig. 45. *Cercis canadensis* (Redbud), × 2/3.

Fig. 46. *Delonix regia* (Royal Poinciana), × 1/2.

7. ENTEROLOBIUM (Earpod Tree)

Trees, unarmed. Leaves bipinnate, pinnae and leaflets in many pairs. Flowers in globose heads, axillary or in short racemes; mostly bisexual; 5-merous; calyx short-dentate; corolla tubular, funnel-shaped, united to the middle; stamens numerous, united into a tube at base. Fruit broadly coiled, thick and compressed, hard, not dehiscent. 10 species. Tropical America and West Indies.

1. **Enterolobium cyclocarpa** (Jacq.) Griseb. (Earpod Tree). Tree to 20 m tall; branches wide-spreading; bark smooth. Leaves with 4 to 15 pairs of pinnae, 10-12 mm long, gland at base of lowest pair. Inflorescence white, sessile, borne on leafy twigs. Fruit 8-11 cm in diameter, dark brown, lustrous. Hammocks and stream banks. Brevard and Pinellas counties. Florida and West Indies. Native of Central America. Escaped from cultivation. Spring. (Fig. 47)

The Earpod Tree grows rapidly, making an excellent shade tree.

8. GLEDITSIA (Honey Locust)

Trees with simple or branched thorns. Leaves deciduous, pinnate to 2-pinnate. Flowers dioecious or polygamous, small, greenish; calyx-lobes obtuse, about as long as petals. Legume flat, stipitate. About 14 species. Tropics and subtropics.

1. **Gleditsia aquatica** Marsh. (Water Locust). Tree to 20 m tall; spines dark red, 7.5-12.5 cm long, simple or with 1 to 3 short branches. Flowers in small clusters on short spikes. Legume 2.5-5 cm long, oval, tips sharp, bases abruptly pointed; usually 1-seeded. River swamps and low hammocks. Sarasota County northward. Florida to Louisiana, Missouri, and South Carolina. Spring. (Fig. 48)

9. LEUCAENA

Trees. Leaves bipinnate; petiolar gland between lowest pinnae or near middle of petiole; leaflets 2-3 mm wide, minutely ciliolate. Flowers in white to pinkish globose heads, solitary or in racemes, axillary; calyx campanulate, dentate; corolla of free petals; stamens 10, free. Legume flat, linear. About 50 species. Mainly tropical America.

1. **Leucaena leucocephala** (Lam.) de Wit. (Jumbie-bean). Leaves glaucous, 4 to 8 pinnae, 8-15 cm long; leaflets falcate, unequal bases, blunt tips. Legume 10-15 cm long, red brown, pulpless, many-seeded. Hammocks and coastal strands. Hillsborough County southward. Florida and West Indies. Summer. *Leucaena glauca* (L.) Benth. (Fig. 49)

Fig. 47. *Enterolobium cyclocarpa* (Earpod Tree), × 1/2.

Descriptive Flora 99

Fig. 48. *Gleditsia aquatica* (Water Locust), × 7/10.

Fig. 49. *Leucaena leucocephala* (Jumbie-bean), × 2/5.

10. PARKINSONIA (Jerusalem Thorn)

Trees or shrubs, armed. Leaves pinnate; leaflets numerous, borne on a phyllodelike rachis. Flowers in racemes; sepals 5; petals 5, spreading, unequal; stamens 10. Legumes torulose, swollen portions nearly terete. 2 species. Tropical, subtropical America and Africa.

1. **Parkinsonia aculeata** L. (Jerusalem Thorn). Branches slender, pendulous. Leaves 20-40 cm long with 1 to 3 pairs of wiry, flattened pinnae. Flowers golden yellow. Legume 10-15 cm long. Hammocks and stream banks. Brevard and Hillsborough counties southward. Florida to South America, also Texas and California. Native of tropical America and Africa. Escaped from cultivation. Spring–summer. (Fig. 50)

11. PISCIDIA (Fishfuddle)

Trees. Leaves alternate with 5 to 9 leaflets. Flowers in short lateral panicles; calyx slightly 2-lipped; petals clawed. Legume narrow with 4 broad wings. 10 species. Florida, Mexico, and West Indies.

1. **Piscidia piscipula** (L.) Sarg. (Jamaica Dogwood). Medium-sized tree. Leaves to 25 cm long, evergreen; leaflets elliptic-ovate. Flowers precede leaves; floral axes and calyx densely puberulent. Flowers silvery-pink (calyx silvery, petals white with red spots). Legume 3-7 cm long, wings thin, lobed, crisped. Coastal strands and hammocks. Hillsborough and Lee counties. Florida to West Indies. Spring. *Ichthyomethia piscipula* (L.) Hitchc. (Fig. 51)

Bark powder from the tree is thrown into the water by fishermen to intoxicate fish or inhibit normal alertness.

12. PITHECELLOBIUM (Blackbead)

Trees or shrubs, unarmed or stipules spinescent. Leaves bipinnate; leaflets small in many pairs or large in few pairs. Flowers in globose heads or cylindric spikes, mostly white, in terminal racemes or solitary or axillary peduncles; sepals 5, united; petals 5, united above middle; stamens numerous, more or less united into a tube. Fruit red, compressed, variously twisted. 90 species. Tropics and subtropics.

1. Leaves coriaceous .... 1. *P. keyense*
1. Leaves chartaceous .... 2. *P. unguis-cati*

1. **Pithecellobium keyense** Britt. ex Britt. & Rose (Blackbead). Leaves with stipular spines or unarmed; leaflets coriaceous, obliquely obovate to elliptic. Filaments pink. Seeds black, with red arils. Coastal

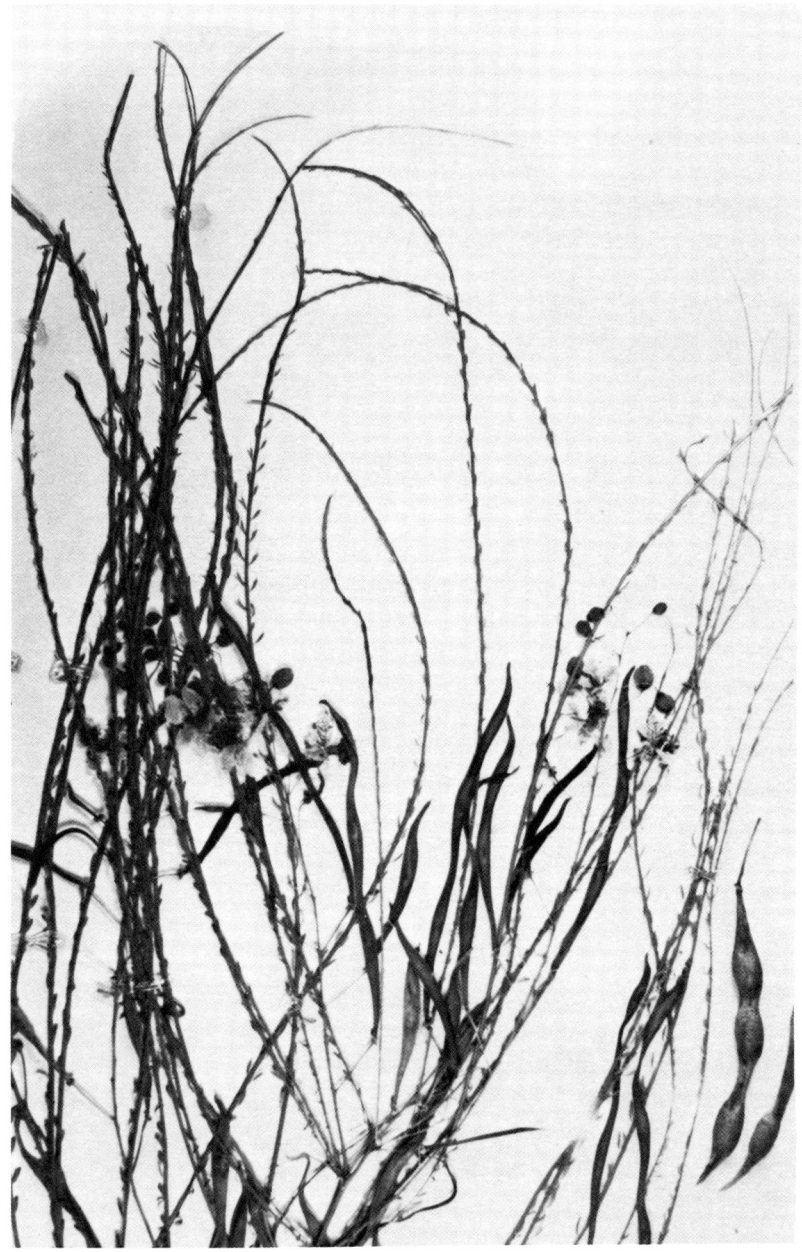

Fig. 50. *Parkinsonia aculeata* (Jerusalem Thorn), × 1/2.

Fig. 51. *Piscidia piscipula* (Jamaica Dogwood), × 3/5.

hammocks. Lee, Palm Beach, and Broward counties. South Florida, Cuba, and the Bahamas.

2. **Pithecellobium unguis-cati** (L.) Benth. (Cat's Claw). Leaves with stipular spines; leaflets chartaceous, obovate to oblong. Filaments pink to yellow. Seeds black, with red arils. Shell mounds, coastal strand. Manatee County southward. Florida and West Indies. *Pithecellobium guadeloupense* (Pers.) Chapm. (Fig. 52)

13. TAMARINDUS (Tamarind)

Trees to 20 m tall; trunk massive to 1.5 m in diameter. Leaves alternate, even-pinnate, 6-12 cm long; leaflets opposite, 10-15 mm long, folding against rachis at night. Flowers in terminal racemes; buds red; calyx-lobes 4; petals unequal, upper 3 yellow gold with red veins; stamens 3. Legumes thick, 6-13 cm long, curved, edges rounded. 1 species. Tropical Africa.

1. **Tamarindus indica** L. (Tamarind). Characters of genus. Coastal strand. Broward and Lee counties. Florida to South America. Native of Africa. Escaped from cultivation. Spring–summer. (Fig. 53)

Tamarind is widely cultivated for its shade and its fruit. It may be eaten fresh or extracted as a flavoring for candy, ice cream, and condiments.

RUTACEAE (Rue Family)

Trees, shrubs, or rarely herbs. Leaves alternate or opposite, simple or compound, usually gland-dotted, glabrous. Flowers bisexual, mostly regular; sepals 3 to 5; petals 3 to 5; stamens equal to or many times the number of petals, usually free; ovary superior, 4 or 5 fused carpels. Fruit baccate, drupaceous or leathery, rarely capsular. 150 genera, 900 species. Tropics and temperate regions.

1. Fruit dry, follicular or samaroid 2
1. Fruit fleshy, drupaceous or baccate 3
    2. Fruit a samara ....3. *Ptelea*
    2. Fruit a follicle ....4. *Zanthoxylum*
3. Fruit a drupe ....1. *Amyris*
3. Fruit a berry ....2. *Citrus*

1. AMYRIS (Torchwood)

Trees or shrubs with resinous, fragrant wood, without spines; branches smooth or pubescent. Leaves usually opposite, odd-pinnate, 3- to 5-foliolate or 1-foliolate. Flowers bisexual in paniculate cymes;

Fig. 52. *Pithecellobium unguis-cati* (Cat's Claw), × 2/3.

Fig. 53. *Tamarindus indica* (Tamarind), × 4/5.

sepals 4 or 5, gland-dotted; petals 4, white; stamens 8 in 2 series inserted at base of disk. Fruit a drupe. 30 species. Tropical and subtropical America.

1. **Amyris elemifera** L. (Torchwood). Characters of genus. Coastal hammocks. Eastern coastal counties in our area. South Florida to West Indies and Central America. All year. (Fig. 54)

Fig. 54. *Amyris elemifera* (Torchwood), × 2/3.

2. CITRUS (Citrus)

Trees or shrubs, often with solitary, axillary spines; young branches frequently armed, older branches unarmed. Leaves alternate, evergreen, 1-foliolate, pellucid-glandular, petiole usually winged. Flowers bisexual, axillary; sepals 4 or 5, united; petals (4-) 5 (-8), white, thick and waxlike; stamens 20 to 60, free or fused, filaments inserted around the disk. Berry with a leathery rind, dotted with oil glands, flesh pulpy, several seeded. 12 species. Tropics and subtropics.

1. Fruits large, orange .... 2. *C. aurantium*
1. Fruits small, greenish yellow .... 1. *C. aurantifolia*

1. **Citrus aurantifolia** (Christm.) Swingle (Key Lime). Small tree or shrub; branches armed with stout spines. Leaves 5-7 cm long, elliptic-ovate, rounded at tip, margins crenate; petioles narrowly winged. Flowers in axillary clusters; petals white; stamens 20 to 25. Fruit about 3-6 cm long, rind thin with 10 segments, pulp greenish yellow, very acid. Hammocks and coastal areas. Coastal counties, rare in the range of this manual. Native of southeast Asia. Florida to tropical America. Spring.

2. **Citrus aurantium** L. (Sour Orange). Tree to 6 m tall; crown rounded; spines long and flexible. Leaves evergreen, 5-11 cm long, 3-5 cm wide, elliptic, acuminate, glandular-punctate; petioles usually broadly winged. Flowers axillary in small cymes; petals white; stamens 20 to 24. Fruit 7-8 cm in diameter, globose with 10 to 12 segments, pulp bittersweet, or very sour. Hammocks, coastal areas. Nearly throughout our area. Native of southeast Asia. Florida to tropical America. Spring. (Fig. 55)

Other **Citrus** species found occasionally in subtropical Florida, rarely escaping or persisting from cultivation: **Citrus paradisi** (L.) Macf. (grapefruit) with large, pale yellow fruit and broadly winged petioles; **Citrus reticulata** Blanco (tangerine) with a rind easily separating from the fruit; **Citrus sinensis** (L.) Osbeck (sweet orange) with sweet pulp and slightly winged petioles; **Citrus limon** (L.) Burm. f. (lemon) with an ovoid fruit with a nipplelike protuberance at the tip; and **Citrus medica** L. (citron) with very thick, rough rind. All are natives of southeast Asia.

3. PTELEA (Hop Tree)

Small trees or shrubs. Leaf blades 3-foliolate, rarely 5-foliolate. Flowers functionally unisexual, sometimes dioecious, in cymes; sepals

Fig. 55. *Citrus aurantium* (Sour Orange), × 7/10.

4 or 5; petals 4 or 5, narrow, greenish. Fruit a samara, nearly orbicular, seed centrally located in a winglike disk, persisting to late autumn. 3 species. North American and Mexico.

1. **Ptelea trifoliata** L. (Hop Tree). Characters of genus. Rich woodlands. Polk County northward. Florida to Texas, Michigan, and New Jersey. Spring. (Fig. 56)

110 TREES OF CENTRAL FLORIDA

Fig. 56. *Ptelea trifoliata* (Hop Tree), × 1/2.

4. ZANTHOXYLUM (Prickly Ash)

Trees or shrubs, often armed with prickles on branches and trunks; bark aromatic. Leaves deciduous or evergreen, alternate, odd- or even-pinnately compound, 3-foliolate or 1-foliolate. Flowers in axillary or terminal spikes, cymes or panicles; sepals none or 3 to 5; petals 3 to 5, white or green; stamens 3 to 5. Fruit of 1 to 5, 2-valved, glandular-punctate follicles. 20 to 30 species. Temperate and subtropical regions.

1. Leaf rachis wing-margined; flowers in axillary spikes ...... .3. *Z. fagara*
1. Leaf rachis not wing-margined; flowers in terminal cymelike panicles 2
   2. Leaflets odd-pinnate, thin, shallowly crenate or serrate .... 1. *Z. clava-herculis*
   2. Leaflets even-pinnate, leathery, entire .... .2. *Z. coriaceum*

   1. **Zanthoxylum clava-herculis** L. (Hercules' Club). Shrub or tree to 17 m tall with many sharp prickles on trunk and young branches. Leaves 1-3 dm long, odd-pinnate with 5 to 19 leaflets, 4-5 cm long, ovate. Flowers unisexual, many, in large terminal cymes; sepals 5; petals 5. Fruit a follicle, 3-5 mm long, subglobose. Hammocks and wet woods. Nearly throughout the range of the manual. Florida to Texas, Arkansas, and Oklahoma. Summer. (Fig. 57)

   2. **Zanthoxylum coriaceum** A. Rich. Shrub or tree to 7 m tall, often armed. Leaves 6-15 cm long, usually even-pinnate; leaflets 6 to 8, rigid, leathery, obovate or elliptic, 3-6 cm long. Flowers unisexual in dense terminal cymes; sepals 3, 1 mm long; petals 3; stamens 3. Fruit a follicle 5-6 mm long. Coastal hammocks. Brevard County southward. South Florida and West Indies. All year.

   3. **Zanthoxylum fagara** (L.) Sarg. (Wild Lime). Shrub or tree to 10 m tall, often with recurved prickles. Leaves 5-11 cm long, odd-pinnate, the rachis winged; leaflets 7 to 9, obovate to ovate, 1-3 cm long. Flowers 4-parted, in short axillary spikes, unisexual, greenish, small. Fruit a follicle, subglobose, 3-4 mm long. Hammocks. Nearly throughout the range of this manual, except central counties. South Florida, Texas, and West Indies. All year.

SIMAROUBACEAE (Quassia Family)

   Trees or shrubs. Leaves alternate, pinnately compound. Flowers small, unisexual or bisexual, in axillary or terminal panicles or cymose racemes; sepals 3 to 7; petals 3 to 7; stamens equal to or twice the number of petals. Fruit a drupe, samara, or baccate. 20 genera, 120 species. Tropics and subtropics.

SIMAROUBA

   Tree with bitter bark. Leaves alternate, even-pinnate, evergreen.

Fig. 57. *Zanthoxylum clava-herculis* (Hercules' Club), × 3/4.

Flowers small, in axillary or terminal panicles; sepals 4 or 5, short; petals 4 or 5, larger than sepals, imbricate; stamens 8 to 10 with fringed appendage at base. Fruit a cluster of 1 to 5 drupes. 40 species. Tropical America.

1. **Simarouba glauca** DC. (Paradise Tree). Leaves 10 to 20, coriaceous, oblong leaflets, 5-10 cm long. Clusters of yellow flowers. Scarlet or purplish fruit. Coastal hammocks. Martin County southward. South Florida, West Indies, Mexico, and South America. Spring. (Fig. 58)

SURIANACEAE (Bay Cedar Family)

Shrub or small tree with gray-pubescent stems. Leaves simple, alternate, entire, linear-spatulate, sessile, fleshy, crowded toward tips of branches. Flowers small, yellow, solitary on in few-flowered clusters; pedicels pubescent; sepals 5, 6-10 mm long; petals 5, 7-10 mm long. Fruit seated in a persistent calyx, 4 or 5 dry sections, pubescent. 1 genus, 1 species. South Florida and West Indies.

1. SURIANA (Bay Cedar)

Characters of the Family

1. **Suriana maritima** L. (Bay Cedar). Characters of the family and genus. Coastal beaches and dunes. Brevard and Pinellas counties southward. South Florida and West Indies. All year. (Fig. 59)

BURSERACEAE

Trees or shrubs. Leaves alternate, pinnately compound, deciduous or evergreen. Flowers generally unisexual, small, in racemes or panicles; sepals 3 to 5; petals 3 to 5, deciduous; stamens twice the number of petals, inserted at the base of the intrastaminal disk. Fruit a drupe or capsule. 16 genera, 500 species. Pantropical.

BURSERA (Torchwood)

Trees or shrubs; bark smooth, exfoliating into thin, reddish flakes; sap strong-scented, resinous. Leaves odd-pinnate, 5 to 13 leaflets, deciduous, obliquely asymmetrical. Staminate flowers 5-parted; pistillate flowers 3-parted. Fruit a reddish drupe that splits into 3 sections. 80 species. Tropical America.

1. **Bursera simaruba** (L.) Sarg. (Gumbo Limbo). Characters of

Fig. 58. *Simarouba glauca* (Paradise Tree), × 1/2.

Descriptive Flora 115

Fig. 59. *Suriana maritima* (Bay Cedar), × 1/2.

genus. Coastal hammocks. Coastal counties from Brevard and Pinellas counties southward. South Florida, West Indies, tropical Central and South Americas. Winter–spring. *Elaphrium simaruba* (L.) Rose (Fig. 60)

All parts of the tree are glutinous, resinous-juicy, scented with turpentine, and yield gum resin. Gumbo Limbo, with its 20 m height and a trunk 1 m in diameter and its smooth, oily-appearing bark, creates a tropical aspect in our subtropical environment.

MELIACEAE (Mahogany Family)

Trees or shrubs. Leaves alternate, blades pinnately compound. Flowers bisexual, in axillary cymes or panicles; sepals 4 to 5, petals 4 to 5 (rarely 3 to 8); stamens 8 to 10, filaments united into a tube; ovary superior. Fruit a berry, capsule, or drupe. 50 genera, 1400 species. Warm regions of the world.

1. Leaves once-pinnately compound, leaflets entire . . . . .2. *Swietenia*
1. Leaves bi- or tri-pinnately compound, leaflets serrate or dentate 1. *Melia*

1. MELIA (Chinaberry)

Trees with variegated wood. Leaves large, once- to tri-pinnately compound; leaflets variously toothed or entire. Flowers in axillary panicles, mostly purplish; sepals 5; petals 5, free and spreading; stamens twice as many as petals; style columnar with 3 to 6 lobes. Fruit a drupe. 2 to 15 species. Subtropics and tropics.

1. **Melia azedarach** L. (Chinaberry). Characters of genus. Flowers fragrant; staminal tube dark purple. Drupe globose, 1-2 cm wide, smooth and yellow, persistent. Disturbed sites, old fields, and in cultivation. Throughout the range of this manual. Florida to Texas, Oklahoma, and Virginia. Native of Asia. Spring. (Fig 61)

2. SWIETENIA (Mahogany)

Trees, with hard wood. Leaves alternate, 1-pinnate. Flowers white; calyx 5-lobed; petals 5, free; stamen tube with 10 anthers; stigma discoid. Fruit a woody capsule with 10 to 14 winged seeds in each cell. 7 or 8 species. Tropical America and West Indies.

1. **Swietenia mahagoni** (L.) Jacq. (Mahogany). Leaflets 4 to 8, evergreen, elliptic to ovate, entire. Capsule ovoid, 6-12 cm long, erect. Coastal hammocks. Known only from Broward County in central Florida. South Florida, West Indies, Central and South America. Spring–summer. (Fig. 62)

Descriptive Flora 117

Fig. 60. *Bursera simaruba* (Gumbo Limbo), × 1/2.

Fig. 61. *Melia azedarach* (Chinaberry), × 3/5.

Descriptive Flora 119

Fig. 62. *Swietenia mahagoni* (Mahogany), × 1/2.

This species is the source of the best mahogany used in cabinetwork.

EUPHORBIACEAE (Spurge Family)

Herbs, shrubs, or trees, often with milky juice, sometimes fleshy and cactuslike. Leaves opposite, whorled or alternate, simple or variously compound; stipules usually present, sometimes reduced to glands, spines, or hairs. Flowers monoecious or occasionally dioecious; calyx and corolla present or absent, when present usually 5-merous; stamens few to many. Fruit a capsule or drupaceous and indehiscent. 300 genera, 5000 species. Cosmopolitan.

1. Leaves evergreen, elliptic, abruptly pointed; fruit drupaceous .... 1. *Drypetes*
1. Leaves deciduous, rhombic-ovate, long-acuminate; fruit a capsule .... 2. *Sapium*

1. DRYPETES

Trees or shrubs. Leaves alternate, leathery, entire or undulate. Flowers apetalous, green or brown; staminate flowers in dense clusters, 4 to 8 sepals, 4 to 16 stamens; pistillate flowers few in a cluster, calyx 4-parted. Fruit a berry or drupe. 200 species. Pantropical.

1. **Drypetes lateriflora** (Sw.) Krug & Urban (Guiana Plum). Shrubs or trees to 10 m tall. Leaves lanceolate to ovate, 8-10 cm long, coriaceous, acute, bases often oblique, margins entire. Drupe red, globose. Hammocks. Brevard County southward. South Florida, Mexico, Central America, and West Indies. Fall. (Fig. 63)

2. SAPIUM (Popcorn Tree)

Trees or shrubs. Leaves alternate, entire, broad. Flowers monoecious in dense spikelike panicles; apetalous; staminate flowers with 2 or 3 sepals and 3 stamens; pistillate flowers with 1 to 5 sepals; ovary 3-celled. Fruit a fleshy capsule; seeds white, remaining attached after capsule walls are shed. 120 species. Tropics and subtropics.

1. **Sapium sebiferum** (L.) Roxb. (Popcorn Tree). Tree to 15 m. Leaves rhombic-ovate, abruptly acuminate. Flowering spike 5-10 cm long. Fruits about 1 cm in diameter. Seeds white, adhering to central column. Hammocks and roadsides. Florida to Louisiana and North Carolina. Escaped from cultivation. Native of East Asia. Spring. *Triadica sebifera* (L.) Small (Fig. 64)

Fig. 63. *Drypetes lateriflora* (Guiana Plum), × 2/5.

122 TREES OF CENTRAL FLORIDA

Fig. 64. *Sapium sebiferum* (Popcorn Tree), × 1/2.

Popcorn tree seeds are coated with fat and yield an oil under pressure.

Jatropha curcas L. (Physic-nut). Persisting from cultivation in coastal areas. Tree to 5 m high. Leaves ovate to slightly 3- to 5-lobed, 5-18 cm wide, petioles as long as blades. Flowers small, yellow. Native of tropical America.

ANACARDIACEAE (Cashew Family)

Trees, shrubs, or vines, usually with resinous bark. Leaves alternate, simple, 3-foliolate or pinnately compound. Inflorescence of racemes or panicles; flowers small, bisexual or unisexual; sepals 3 to 5, green; petals 3 to 5, greenish yellow to white; stamens twice as many as petals; ovary superior. Fruit a drupe. 60 genera, 600 species. Chiefly pantropical.

1. Leaves simple .... 1. *Mangifera*
1. Leaves pinnately compound 2
   2. Leaflets most 11 to 23 .... 2. *Rhus*
   2. Leaflets 5 to 9 3
3. Mature leaflets over 4 cm wide, bases truncate;
   fruit yellow brown .... 2. *Metopium*
3. Mature leaflets less than 4 cm wide, bases cuneate to attenuate;
   fruit red .... 4. *Schinus*

1. MANGIFERA (Mango)

Medium to large trees. Leaves alternate, petiolate, evergreen. Flowers in terminal, branching panicles; calyx 4- to 5-parted; petals 4 to 5, spreading; stamens 1 to 5, inserted on the margin of the disk; ovary compressed, style lateral and curved. Fruit a drupe, reniform or ovoid, fleshy. About 40 species. Tropical Asia.

1. **Mangifera indica** L. (Mango). Trees to 15 m. Leaves 10-20 cm long, linear-lanceolate or narrowly elliptic, glabrous, acute or acuminate. Flowers whitish green or yellowish green; sepals ovate, 2-3 mm long; petals elliptic, 5 mm long; fertile stamens 1 or 2. Drupe varying in size and color. Widely cultivated tree. Persistent around old homesites and occasionally naturalized. Native of South Asia. Spring. (Fig. 65)

2. METOPIUM (Poisonwood)

Shrubs or trees. Leaves evergreen, stout-petiolate, odd-pinnate, clustered near tips of branches. Flowers dioecious, in open axillary panicles; sepals 5, fused; petals 5, twice the length of the sepals; stamens 5; stigma 3-lobed. Fruit drupaceous, oblong to obovate, glabrous, shining. 3 species. South Florida, West Indies, Mexico, and South America.

1. **Metopium toxiferum** (L.) Krug & Urban (Poisonwood). Characters of genus. Resinous, milky, caustic sap. Evergreen leaves with 3 to 7 leathery, ovate leaflets, 3-9 cm long. Orange fruit in drooping clusters. Hammocks, pinelands, and sand dunes. Martin

Fig. 65. *Mangifera indica* (Mango), × 2/5.

County southward. South Florida and West Indies. Spring. (Fig. 66) All parts of the tree act as a contact skin poison to many people.

3. RHUS (Sumac)

Trees or shrubs. Leaves alternate, pinnately compound. Flowers usually monoecious, in dense terminal panicles; sepals 4 to 5, green; petals 4 to 5, greenish yellow or white; stamens 4 to 5. Fruit a pubescent drupe; seeds smooth. 250 species. Subtropical and warm regions.

Descriptive Flora 125

Fig. 66. *Metopium toxiferum* (Poisonwood), × 2/5.

1. Inflorescence terminal fruit red ....1. *R. copallina*
1. Inflorescence axillary; fruit white to greenish white ....2. *R. vernix*

1. **Rhus copallina** L. (Winged Sumac). Dioecious shrubs or trees to 10 m tall; bark covered with large, red brown excrescences that separate into large, thin, papery scales. Leaflet blades acuminate, elliptic, 3-10 cm long; leaf rachis winged. Flowers small, in dense terminal clusters as long as the leaves. Fruit pubescent, lustrous, red,

ovate. Dry hillsides and pinelands. Throughout central Florida. Florida to Texas, Minnesota to Maine. Spring. *Rhus leucantha* Jacq; *Rhus obtusifolia* Small (Fig. 67)

2. **Rhus vernix** L. (Poison Sumac). Shrub or tree, 3 to 7 m tall; bark smooth. Leaflet blades elliptic, 4-15 cm long, undulate; become conspicuously red and yellow in fall. Flowers very small, yellowish, in open clusters in leaf axils. Fruits ivory white or yellowish, about 5 mm broad, subglobose, in drooping panicles. Swamps and wet woods. Rare in central Florida. Marion County northward to Louisiana, Minnesota, and Maine. Spring. *Toxicodendron vernix* (L.) Kuntze

4. SCHINUS (Pepper Tree) (Brazilian Pepper Tree)

Small trees or shrubs, dioecious. Leaves alternate, odd-pinnate, resinous. Flowers unisexual, bracteate, in terminal or axillary panicles; calyx 5-parted; petals 5, white, longer than sepals; stamens 10 in 2 series. Fruit a globose drupe. 30 species. Temperate and tropical America.

1. **Schinus terebinthifolius** Raddi (Brazilian Pepper Tree). Characters of genus. Leaves to 15 cm long, usually 7 leaflets, glabrous. Drupes glabrous, pinkish red, resinous, maturing in winter. Mangrove associations and along streams and canals. Throughout central Florida. Native of tropical America. Spring. (Fig. 68)

This species is an aggressive invader and is difficult to eradicate.

CYRILLACEAE (Titi Family)

Shrubs or small trees. Leaves evergreen, simple, alternate, entire, glabrous. Inflorescences terminal or in axillary racemes, flowers small, regular, perfect; calyx (4-) 5 (-8)-parted; petals as many as sepals, white or pinkish white; stamens 5 to 10; ovary superior. Fruit a dry, terete or winged, nutlike drupe. 3 genera, 14 species. American.

1. CYRILLA (Titi)

Shrubs or small trees to 10 m. Leaves 5-10 cm long, often clustered toward ends of branches; blades veiny at maturity. Flowers in groups of 6 to 10 lateral racemes; sepals 5, separate, white, lanceolate, keeled; petals 5, lanceolate, acute; stamens 5, equal, inserted at base of corolla; stigma 2- to 4-lobed. Fruit ovoid, drupaceous, brown or olive. 1 species. Southeastern United States.

1. **Cyrilla racemiflora** L. (Titi). Characters of genus. Swamps, wet

Fig. 67. *Rhus copallina* (Winged Sumac), × 3/5.

Fig. 68. *Schinus terebinthifolius* (Brazilian Pepper Tree), × 2/5.

pinelands, and dry sand dunes. Highlands County northward. Florida to Texas and Virginia. Spring–summer. *Cyrilla arida* Small; *Cyrilla parviflora* Raf. (Fig. 69)

AQUIFOLIACEAE (Holly Family)

Trees or shrubs. Leaves entire or toothed. Flowers bisexual or

Fig. 69. *Cyrilla racemiflora* (Titi), × 1/2.

unisexual, radially symmetrical, in axillary cymes or solitary; sepals 4 to 9, small, imbricate; petals 4 to 9, inconspicuous; stamens equal in number and alternate with petals; ovary superior. Fruit drupaceous. 3 genera, about 312 species. Old and New World.

1. ILEX (Holly)

Trees or shrubs. Leaves simple, petiolate; stipules minute, deciduous. Flowers small, white or greenish, solitary or cymose in axillary clusters, pistillate with nonfunctional stamens, staminate with rudimentary pistil; calyx 4- to 9-lobed; petals 4 to 9; stamens adnate to corolla tube; style usually wanting; stigmas 2 to 10, distinct or united. Fruit a berry. 300 species. 15 indigenous to North America.

1. Leaves coriaceous, evergreen 2
1. Leaves chartaceous to subcoriaceous, deciduous 4
   2. Leaves crenate throughout their length .... 5. *I. vomitoria*
   2. Leaves serrate, dentate or entire 3
3. Leaves spinulose-dentate or entire; teeth or at least the apex armed with a rigid spine, 1 mm long or more .... 4. *I. opaca*
3. Leaves spinulose-serrate or entire; teeth (if present) and apex unarmed or with a spine less than 1 mm long .... 2. *I. cassine*
   4. Leaves crenate, tapering to narrow cuneate base ...... 3. *I. decidua*
   4. Leaves serrate, rounded or with a broad cuneate base .1. *I. ambigua*

1. **Ilex ambigua** (Michx.) Torr. (Carolina Holly). Shrub or small tree to 6 m; branches glabrous to densely pubescent. Leaves deciduous, ovate to elliptic, 3-18 cm long, 1.5-7 cm wide, acute to acuminate at apex. Inflorescences axillary, staminate flowers 2 to 8, pistillate flowers 1 to 3. Fruit red, subglobose, 4-12 mm diameter. Sandy, upland woods and hammocks. Throughout central Florida. Florida to Texas, Arkansas, North Carolina. Spring.

2. **Ilex cassine** L. (Dahoon). Shrub or small tree to 12 m; branches puberulent or glabrate. Leaves evergreen, elliptic to ovate, 3-14 cm long, 2-5 cm wide, revolute. Inflorescences axillary, staminate flowers numerous, pistillate flowers 1 to 9. Fruit red, orange, or yellow, subglobose, 6-9 mm diameter. Flatwood depressions and along edges of ponds and swamps. Throughout Florida to Texas and Virginia. Spring. (Fig. 70)

3. **Ilex decidua** Walt. (Possum Haw). Shrub or small tree to 10 m; branches glabrous or pubescent. Leaves deciduous, oblanceolate, or spatulate, 2.5-8 cm long, 0.8-4.5 cm wide. Inflorescences axillary, not pedunculate; staminate and pistillate flowers 1 to 3. Fruits red, orange,

Fig. 70. *Ilex cassine* (Dahoon), × 2/5.

or yellow, subglobose, 4-9 mm diameter. Upland alluvial woods and thickets. Gulf coastal areas from DeSoto County northward. Florida to Texas, Kansas, and Maryland. Spring.

4. **Ilex opaca** Ait. (American Holly). Shrub or small tree to 15 m; branches pubescent to glabrate. Leaves deciduous, ovate, elliptic to oblanceolate, 3.5-10 cm long, 1.5-5 cm wide, revolute. Inflorescences axillary, staminate flowers 3 to 10, pistillate flowers 1 to 3. Fruits red, orange, or yellow, subglobose, 7-12 mm diameter. Mesic woodlands. Hillsborough County northward. Florida to Texas, Oklahoma, and Massachusetts. Spring.

Commonly cultivated as an ornamental tree in eastern North

America and Europe. Its foliage and red berries are used as Christmas decorations.

5. **Ilex vomitoria** Ait. (Yaupon). Shrub or small tree to 8 m; branches pubescent. Leaves evergreen, oval to elliptic, 1-4.5 cm long, 0.8-2 cm wide, obtuse at apex, broadly cuneate at base; revolute. Inflorescences axillary; staminate flowers 4 to 10, short pedunculate; pistillate flowers 1 to 3, subsessile. Fruits red, subglobose, 5-7 mm diameter. Sandy, upland and maritime woods. Sarasota County northward. Florida to Texas, Arkansas, and Virginia. Spring.

The leaves of **Ilex vomitoria** contain caffeine. An infusion of the leaves is reported to have been used by Southern Indians as a ceremonial drink. This species is commonly used as an evergreen hedge.

CELASTRACEAE (Bittersweet Family)

Trees, shrubs, or climbing vines. Leaves simple, alternate or opposite. Flowers cymose or fasciculate, bisexual, radially symmetrical; calyx 4- to 5-lobed; petals 5; stamens 4 to 5, alternate with petals and inserted on or below a well-marked disk that is often flat and fleshy; ovary superior. Fruit a capsule, drupe, or berry. 55 genera, 850 species. Temperate and tropical regions.

1. MAYTENUS (Mayten)

Shrubs or small trees; branches smooth. Leaves evergreen, coriaceous, alternate. Flowers small, polygamous, axillary, cymose or solitary; calyx 5-parted; petals 5, spreading; stamens 5, inserted below the disk; ovary immersed in disk; stigma 2- to 4-lobed. Fruit a capsule. 225 species. Subtropical.

1. **Maytenus phyllanthoides** Benth. (Gutta-percha). Leaves ashy gray, glabrous, broadly oblanceolate, 2-5.5 cm long. Mature capsule with 3 or 4 arillate seeds, 3 mm long. Coastal hammocks. Levy County southward along Gulf Coast. Florida to West Indies and tropical America. Spring–summer. (Fig. 71)

ACERACEAE (Maple Family)

Trees or shrubs. Leaves opposite, palmately lobed, simple, or pinnately compound. Flowers in fascicles, bisexual or unisexual; sepals 4 or 5; petals 4 or 5 or absent; disk present; stamens 4 to 10, usually 8; ovary superior. Fruit a 2-winged samara. About 3 genera, 200 species. North temperate and tropical montane.

Descriptive Flora 133

Fig. 71. *Maytenus phyllanthoides* (Gutta-percha), × 1/2.

1. ACER (Maple)

Deciduous trees or shrubs. Leaves usually palmately 3- to 9-lobed or pinnately compound with 3 to 5 leaflets. Flowers polygamous or unisexual, in terminal or axillary racemes, corymbs or fascicles; sepals (4-) 5 (-12); petals absent or (4-) 5 (-12); stamens 4 to 10, inserted on a disk; stigmas 2; ovary superior, compressed. Fruit a 2-winged samara, each wing with 1 seed. About 200 species. North temperate and tropical montane.

1. Leaves compound, leaflets 3 to 7 ....1. *A. negundo*
1. Leaves simple 2
   2. Flowers in axillary clusters, appearing before leaves 3
   2. Flowers in terminal corymbs, appearing
      with leaves ....4. *A. saccharum*
3. Leaves cut less than halfway to main vein at base,
   typically 3-lobed; petals present, similar to sepals ....2. *A. rubrum*
3. Leaves cut more than halfway to main vein at base;
   petals absent ....3. *A. saccharinum*

    1. **Acer negundo** L. (Box Elder). Tree to 20 m tall. Leaflets ovate or elliptic, 5-12 cm long, coarsely toothed. Staminate flowers in fascicles, sepals 0.5-1 mm long, anthers pubescent, drooping; pistillate flowers in racemes, sepals 1.5 mm long. Fruit a samara, 2.5-3.5 cm long. Moist woods and stream banks. Osceola County northward. Florida to Texas, Michigan, and Maine. Spring. *Negundo negundo* (L.) Karst.

    Plants in the range of the manual belong to **Acer negundo** subspecies **latifolium** (Pax) Schwerin.

    2. **Acer rubrum** L. (Southern Red Maple). Tree to 30 m tall; bark dark gray and fissured on trunk. Leaves variable in size and shape, palmately 3- to 5-lobed, acuminate, serrate, base rounded or cordate. Staminate and pistillate flowers in clusters, red to scarlet. Winged fruit scarlet, brownish red or straw colored, 1.5-3.5 cm long. Moist woods and swamps. Throughout Florida to Texas and Maine. Winter–spring. *Rufacer carolinianum* Walt.; *Rufacer rubrum* (L.) Small. Our plants belong to **Acer rubrum** var. **trilobum** K. Koch. (Fig. 72)

    3. **Acer saccharinum** L. (Silver Maple). Tree to 30 m tall, slender, typically with several upright, secondary trunks from the principal one. Leaves deeply 5-lobed, to 1.5 dm long and wide, undersurface white or silvery. Staminate and pistillate flowers small, in dense clusters; pistillate sepals yellow to rose. Fruits straw colored, 5-7.5 cm long, body thick. Wet woods. Rare in central Florida, but often cultivated as an

Fig. 72. *Acer rubrum* (Southern Red Maple), × 1/2.

ornamental. Northern Florida to Louisiana, North Dakota, and Maine. Winter–spring. *Argenter saccharinum* (L.) Small

4. **Acer saccharum** Marsh. (Southern Sugar Maple). Tree of medium height; dead and brown foliage persists through winter. Leaves 3- to 5-lobed, to 15 cm long and 18 cm wide, acute or acuminate, lobes often lobed, base truncate to cordate. Flowers small, clustered, greenish yellow, pedicels filiform; petals absent. Fruit a samara, reddish brown, 3.5-4 cm long. Moist rich woods. Northwest counties in central Florida. Florida to Texas and Maine. Spring–fall. *Saccharodendron barbatum* (Michx.) Nieuwl; *Saccharodendron floridanum* (Chapm.) Nieuwl.

Plants in the range of this manual belong to **Acer saccharum** subspecies **floridanum** (Chapm.) Desm. The long, straight trunks make this tree useful for flooring and furniture.

HIPPOCASTANACEAE (Horse-Chestnut Family)

Trees or shrubs. Leaves opposite, blades palmately compound. Flowers polygamous, in terminal racemes or panicles; sepals 5, partially united; petals 4 or 5, unequal, clawed; stamens 5 to 8. Fruit a leathery capsule. 2 genera, 15 species. North temperate regions.

1. AESCULUS (Buckeye)

Tree or shrubs. Leaves deciduous, large, opposite, palmately compound; leaflets 5 to 7, lanceolate to obovate, irregularly serrate; petioles 5-15 cm long. Staminate and perfect flowers in terminal panicles; calyx 5-lobed, subcylindric, villous; petals 4, separate, unequal, clawed; stamens 5 to 8; ovary superior. Fruit a smooth, leathery capsule; seeds tan to dark brown with a prominent pale scar, 1-2.5 cm diameter. 13 species. North America, Europe, and Asia.

1. **Aesculus pavia** L. (Red Buckeye). Characters of genus. Small tree to 6 m tall. Leaflets 6-17 cm long, 3-6 cm wide; petals scarlet, margins glandular. Swamp margins and wet pinelands. Seminole County northward. Florida to Texas, Missouri, and Virginia. Spring. (Fig. 73)

SAPINDACEAE (Soapberry Family)

Trees, shrubs, or woody climbers. Leaves alternate, simple or compound. Flowers bisexual or unisexual, often small, inconspicuous, in racemes or panicles; sepals 4 or 5, free or fused; petals 4 or 5 or absent; stamens 6 to 12, inserted within or on disk; ovary superior. Fruit capsular or baccate. 150 genera, 2000 species. Tropics and subtropics.

1. Leaflets 7 to 13, lanceolate, acuminate .... 2. *Sapindus*
1. Leaflets 2 to 4 (-6), elliptic, obtuse .... 1. *Exothea*

1. EXOTHEA

Shrubs or trees. Leaves evergreen, alternate, pinnately compound or appearing simple. Flowers small, in axillary panicles; calyx 5-parted, persistent; petals 5, white; stamens 7 to 10 (mostly 8) inserted on fleshy disk. Fruit a berry, globose, 1-seeded. 3 species. Tropical America.

Fig. 73. *Aesculus pavia* (Red Buckeye), × 2/5.

1. **Exothea paniculata** (Juss.) Radlk. (Inkwood). Trees up to 12 m tall. Leaves 2- to 4-foliolate, or appearing 1-foliolate and simple. Flowers clustered at ends of branches. Fruit subglobose, 1 cm wide, orange, turning dark purple. Hammocks and shell mounds. Volusia County southward along east coast in our area. Florida to Central America and West Indies. Winter–spring. (Fig. 74)

2. SAPINDUS (Soapberry)

Shrubs or trees. Leaves alternate, pinnately compound. Flowers

Fig. 74. *Exothea paniculata* (Inkwood), × 2/5.

monoecious or dioecious, in terminal racemes or panicles; sepals 4 or 5, unequal; petals 4 or 5, equal, white or greenish; stamens 8 to 10. Fruit drupelike, 1-seeded, resinous. 13 species. Tropics and subtropics.

1. Leaf rachis not winged .... 1. *S. marginatus*
1. Leaf rachis winged .... 2. *S. saponaria*

1. **Sapindus marginatus** Willd. (Florida Soapberry). Tree to 10 m tall; short buttressed trunks. Leaves deciduous, alternate, pinnately compound, 6 to 14 leaflets, 8-10 cm long. Flowers greenish, in terminal panicles. Fruit pale yellow-brown, 3-lobed, globose. Hammocks. Lee County northward to Georgia. Spring. Sometimes not considered distinct from and merged with the next species. (Fig. 75)

2. **Sapindus saponaria** L. (Soapberry). Trees up to 15 m tall; broad dense crowns. Leaves pinnate, leaflets 6 to 12, lanceolate to oblong, 6-18 cm long, obtuse to long-acuminate, asymmetric; leaf rachis winged. Flowers white in much-branched panicles. Fruit globose, 1-2 cm wide, fleshy; seeds pale, 1 cm diameter. Hammocks. Lee County southward to Mexico and tropical America. All year.

RHAMNACEAE (Buckthorn Family)

Trees, shrubs, or climbing vines; branches often thorny. Leaves simple, pinnately veined. Flowers bisexual or unisexual, small, in cymose inflorescences; calyx 4- to 5-lobed, tubular or cup-shaped; petals 4 or 5, cupped or hooded, or absent; stamens 4 or 5, alternate to sepals, anthers fitting into hood of the petals; disk present; ovary free or sunken in the disk. Fruit capsular, berrylike or drupaceous. 58 genera, 900 species. Cosmopolitan.

1. Leaves subopposite; fruit drupaceous, pulpy .... 1. *Krugiodendron*
1. Leaves alternate; fruit berrylike or dry .... 2. *Rhamnus*

1. KRUGIODENDRON (Leadwood)

Trees or shrubs up to 10 m tall. Leaves evergreen, opposite, entire, ovate or elliptic, 3-7 cm long, dark green above, paler beneath. Flowers bisexual, small, yellowish green, in axillary, cymose inflorescences; calyx 5-parted, lobes longer than tube; petals absent; stamens 5, disk annular. Fruit a small ovoid drupe, black, 5-8 mm long. 1 species. Florida, Mexico, Central America, and West Indies.

1. **Krugiodendron ferreum** (Vahl) Urban (Black Ironwood). Characters of genus. Tropical hammock forests. East coastal counties. Florida to Mexico, Central America, and West Indies. Spring. (Fig. 76)

140 TREES OF CENTRAL FLORIDA

Fig. 75. *Sapindus marginatus* (Florida Soapberry), × 1/2.

Fig. 76. *Krugiodendron ferreum* (Black Ironwood), × 7/10.

The very close-grained hardwood is the heaviest hardwood in the United States.

2. RHAMNUS (Buckthorn)

Trees or shrubs. Leaves alternate, entire or serrate, deciduous, prominently veined, 10-15 cm long, elliptic. Flowers small, bisexual, 5-merous, solitary or in short-peduncled, axillary clusters; stamens 4 or 5, included. Fruit a globose drupe, 1 cm diameter, red in summer, shiny black at maturity. 110 species. Cosmopolitan.

1. **Rhamnus caroliniana** Walt. (Carolina Buckthorn). Characters of genus. Calyx campanulate, 3-4 mm long, lobes 5, lanceolate; petals shorter than calyx. Moist deciduous woods. Orange County northward. Florida to Texas, Kansas, and Virginia. Spring–fall. (Fig. 77)

ELEOCARPACEAE (Eleocarpus Family)

Trees or shrubs. Leaves alternate or opposite. Flowers bisexual, in racemes, panicles, or cymes; sepals 4 or 5; petals 4 or 5 or absent; stamens many, adnate to disk. Fruit a capsule or drupe. 12 genera, 350 species. Tropics and subtropics.

1. MUNTINGIA (Strawberry Tree)

Trees or shrubs to 12 m tall. Leaves 6-14 cm long, oblong-lanceolate, acuminate, base oblique, irregularly or coarsely serrate, smooth above, densely gray or white stellate-pubescent below. Flowers large, 1-flowered on axillary peduncles or in sessile clusters of 2 or 3; sepals 5; petals 5, white, about 1 cm long; stamens many, free, inserted on an annular disk; ovary with glandular hairs. Fruit a berry, smooth, subglobose, 1 cm wide, red or yellow. 3 species. South American and West Indies.

1. **Muntingia calabura** L. (Strawberry Tree). Characters of genus. Disturbed hammocks and pinelands. Hendry County southward. Florida, Mexico, West Indies, and South America. Native to tropical America. Escaped from cultivation. Spring–fall. (Fig. 78)

TILIACEAE (Linden Family)

Trees, shrubs, or herbs. Leaves simple, alternate or rarely opposite. Flowers bisexual, cymose; sepals 5; petals 5, free; stamens many; ovary superior. Fruit baccate or a drupaceous capsule. 50 genera, 450 species. Tropical and temperate regions.

1. TILIA (Basswood)

Trees. Leaves deciduous, widely ovate to suborbicular, to 20 cm long, glabrate to stellate-tomentose, acuminate, serrate, base cordate, oblique or truncate, long-petioled. Flowers bisexual in axillary cymes; peduncle adnate to a coriaceous or membranous, foliaceous bract; sepals 5, pubescent inside; petals 5, yellow or cream colored; stamens numerous, in clusters; ovary superior. Fruit brown, woody, nutlike,

Descriptive Flora 143

Fig. 77. *Rhamnus caroliniana* (Carolina Buckthorn), × 1/2.

144 Trees of Central Florida

Fig. 78. *Muntingia calabura* (Strawberry Tree), × 1/2.

sometimes ribbed, globose, 5-9 mm diameter. 50 species. North temperate regions and Mexico.

1. **Tilia caroliniana** Mill. (Carolina Basswood). Characters of genus. Young twigs tomentose or tomentose-hirsute; fascicles of trichomes on leaves more than 0.5 mm broad. Moist woods. Northern half of central Florida. Florida to Texas, Arkansas, and North Carolina. Spring–summer. *Tilia truncata* Spach; *Tilia floridana* Small; *Tilia australis* Small; *Tilia leucocarpa* Ashe; *Tilia littoralis* Sarg.; *Tilia georgiana* Sarg; *Tilia porracea* Ashe (Fig. 79)

MALVACEAE (Mallow Family)

Trees, shrubs, or herbs. Leaves alternate, simple, often palmately lobed. Flowers bisexual, axillary, solitary or racemose; sepals 5, united at base more than one-half the length; petals 5, united at base; stamens united by their filaments into a long column; style branched above the column. Fruit dry, capsular, rarely a berry or samara. 75 genera, 1000 species. Tropical and temperate regions.

1. HIBISCUS (Rose Mallow)

Trees, shrubs, or herbs. Leaves entire, lobed or parted. Flowers solitary or in racemes or panicles; involucel bracts several, rarely 3 to 5; bractlets distinct; calyx campanulate, 5-lobed or toothed; corolla rotate, petals 5; style branches 5, stigmas capitate or flattened. Fruit a 5-valved capsule. 3000 species. Tropics and subtropics.

1. **Hibiscus tiliaceus** L. (Mahoe). Characters of genus. Tree, evergreen, to 6 m tall. Leaves cordate, nearly round, abruptly pointed, densely stellate-tomentose beneath. Flowers large, yellow, becoming red. Fruit a silky, 5-parted capsule. Shore hammocks. Coastal areas. Florida to Mexico, Central and South America, West Indies. Escaped from cultivation. Spring. *Pariti tiliaceum* (L.) St. Hil. (Fig. 80)

THEACEAE (Tea Family)

Trees or shrubs. Leaves simple, alternate. Flowers showy, bisexual, axillary, solitary; sepals 5, imbricate; petals 5; stamens numerous, adnate to petals; ovary superior. Fruit a woody capsule. 16 genera, 50 species. Tropical and temperate regions.

1. GORDONIA (Loblolly Bay)

Trees. Leaves evergreen, leathery, marginal teeth appressed and

Fig. 79. *Tilia caroliniana* (Carolina Basswood), × 2/5.

Descriptive Flora 147

Fig. 80. *Hibiscus tiliaceus* (Mahoe), × 3/5.

blunt, lower surface glabrous. Flowers long-pedicelled, axillary, solitary; sepals 5; petals 5; stamens borne on a 5-lobed disk. Fruit a capsule. 40 species. America and Asia.

1. **Gordonia lasianthus** (L.) Ellis (Loblolly Bay). Characters of genus. Flowers to 7.5 cm in diameter, pure white, silky on back; petals fringed and with broadly rounded tips turned up; stamens yellow, clustered. Bayheads, swamps. Glades County northward. Florida to Louisiana and North Carolina. (Fig. 81)

Fig. 81. *Gordonia lasianthus* (Loblolly Bay), × 3/5.

CARICACEAE (Papaya Family)

Small trees and shrubs; milky juice. Leaves alternate, simple, terminal, large, palmately lobed. Flowers bisexual or unisexual, racemose; staminate flowers small, calyx 5-lobed, petals fused, stamens 10 in 2 series, epipetalous; pistillate flowers subsessile with 5-lobed calyx, petals free; ovary superior. Fruit a many-seeded, pulpy berry, globose or pyriform. 4 genera, 55 species. Tropical Africa and America.

1. CARICA (Papaya)

Small trees or shrubs with simple stems. Leaves long-petioled, simple, deeply lobed. Flowers axillary, cymose or racemose, dioecious; staminate corolla with slender tube, lobes contorted in bud, stamens 10, inserted in throat of corolla; pistillate corolla linear-oblong, style very short, stigmas 5, linear or cleft. Fruit a fleshy berry. About 45 species. Warm America.

1. **Carica papaya** L. (Papaya). Characters of genus. Tree to 6 m tall; trunk hollow, soft, marked with scars of fallen leaves. Staminate flowers in pedunculate panicles 10-30 cm long; pistillate in short, 3-flowered cymes, corolla longer than in staminate flowers. Berry variable, small and ovoid in wild plants. Hammocks, shell mounds, and disturbed sites. Hillsborough County southward. Florida to West Indies. Cultivated throughout the tropics. Native of tropical America. Escaped from cultivation. All year. (Fig. 82)

The juice of the fruit and leaves contains an enzyme, papain, which is used to tenderize meat. The fruit is edible.

RHIZOPHORACEAE (Mangrove Family)

Trees or shrubs. Leaves evergreen, coriaceous, opposite, entire or toothed, petioled. Flowers bisexual; calyx tube fused to ovary, 3- to 14-cleft, valvate, persistent; petals as many as sepals; inserted on disk; ovary inferior. Fruit leathery, crowned with calyx. 16 genera, 120 species. Pantropical.

1. RHIZOPHORA (Mangrove)

Trees; aerial roots arising from the trunk and branches at base of plant. Leaves evergreen, smooth, opposite, leathery. Flowers 2 to several in peduncled clusters, nodding; calyx tube 4-parted, subtended by

Fig. 82. *Carica papaya* (Papaya), × 3/5.

2 bracts; petals 4, stamens 8 to 12. Fruit pendulous, leathery, ovoid. 7 species. Pantropical.

1. **Rhizophora mangle** L. (Red Mangrove). Characters of genus. Tree to 25 m tall, usually smaller; bark gray, red within. Leaves 5-15 cm long, thick, obovate to elliptic, obtuse, entire; stipules 2.5-4 cm long. Tidal swamps. Coastal counties. Florida to tropical America. All year. (Fig. 83)

The long, cylindrical fruit contains the seedling that begins elongating while still on the tree. If a seedling falls on muddy soil, it roots and grows. If it falls into the water, it floats in the perpendicular position until stranded and striking root. Red mangrove, with its

Descriptive Flora 151

Fig. 83. *Rhizophora mangle* (Red Mangrove), × 2/5.

stiltlike rootlets, prevents erosion and, by collecting debris at its base, eventually extends the coastline.

COMBRETACEAE (Combretum Family)

Trees, shrubs, or vines. Leaves simple, opposite or alternate, leathery. Flowers bisexual or unisexual, in spikes or racemes; calyx tube fused to ovary, 4 to 8 lobes; petals 4 or 5 or none; stamens 4 to 10; ovary inferior. Fruit usually winged, indehiscent. 19 genera, 600 species. Tropics and subtropics.

1. Leaves alternate; fruits scalelike; imbricated in conelike clusters .... 1. *Conocarpus*
1. Leaves opposite; fruit obovoid, solitary .... 2. *Laguncularia*

1. CONOCARPUS (Buttonwood)

Trees or shrubs. Leaves evergreen. Flowers bisexual, small, in dense, conelike heads, terminal panicles; calyx tube 5-toothed; petals absent; stamens 5, anthers cordate. Fruit small, densely clustered together. 2 species. Mangrove swamps of America and West Africa.

1. **Conocarpus erecta** L. (Buttonwood). Characters of genus. Trees to 6 m tall, usually shrubs. Smooth or silky foliage. Fruits purplish green, conelike. Coastal swamps, hammocks, and sandy shores. Coastal counties. Florida to tropical America. All year. *Conocarpus erecta* var. *sericea* Forst. ex DC. (Fig. 84)

2. LAGUNCULARIA (White Mangrove)

Trees or shrubs; roots with small pneumatophores. Leaves opposite, coriaceous, succulent with 2 conspicuous glands at base of petiole. Flowers polygamous in axillary, pubescent, simple or branched spikes; calyx tube 5-toothed, persistent, urceolate; petals 5, minute; stamens 10. Fruit ovoid. 2 species. Tropical America and Africa.

1. **Laguncularia racemosa** (L.) Gaertn. f. (White Mangrove). Characters of the genus. Brackish, coastal swamps. Coastal counties. Florida to tropical America. Spring. (Fig. 85)

White mangrove is usually found on higher ground than other mangrove species.

MYRTACEAE (Myrtle Family)

Trees or shrubs. Leaves evergreen, simple, entire, opposite or rarely alternate. Flowers bisexual; calyx fused to ovary, 3- to 5- (-many)

Fig. 84. *Conocarpus erecta* (Buttonwood), × 1/2.

Fig. 85. *Laguncularia racemosa* (White Mangrove), × 1/2.

lobed; petals 4 or 5 or none, inserted on margins of disk; stamens many, free or fused at the base into a short tube, or in bundles opposite the petals; ovary inferior. Fruit a capsule, berrylike, or a drupe. 100 genera, 3000 species. Pantropical.

1. Leaves alternate, with 3 to 8 parallel veins; fruit dry ...... 2. *Melaleuca*
1. Leaves opposite, pinnately veined; fruit fleshy 2
   2. Fruit a many-seeded berry .... 4. *Psidium*
   2. Fruit a 1- to 2-seeded berry 3
3. Inflorescences cymose .... 3. *Myrcianthes*
3. Inflorescences racemose, fasciculate, or flower solitary ..... 1. *Eugenia*

1. EUGENIA (Stopper)

Trees or shrubs. Leaves opposite, ovate, narrowed at apex, pinnately veined, glandular dotted on lower surface. Flowers white; inflorescence variable, sessile or short-peduncled; sepals broad; petals 4, white, ovate to orbicular; stamens many. Berry crowned by persistent lobes of calyx. 1000 species. Tropics and subtropics.

1. Pedicels over 5 mm long, slender 2
1. Pedicels less than 5 mm long, stout 3
   2. Fruits 2-3 cm in diameter, orange red; calyx-lobes lanceolate,
      leaflike, in 2 equal parts .... 4. *E. uniflora*
   2. Fruits 7-8 mm in diameter, black; calyx-lobes reniform,
      not leaflike, in 2 unequal pairs .... 3. *E. rhombea*
3. Leaves oblanceolate (rarely elliptic), apex rounded or obtuse 2. *E. foetida*
3. Leaves ovate or lanceolate (rarely elliptic), apex acute .... 1. *E. axillaris*

   1. **Eugenia axillaris** (Sw.) Willd. (White Stopper). Small tree or shrub up to 7 m tall; bark scaly. Leaves 3-7 cm long, base cuneate or acute, bluntly acuminate, slightly paler beneath than above. Flowers conspicuous in axillary clusters; calyx-lobes in 2 unequal pairs; petals white, 2-3 mm long; stamens about 40. Fruit a bluish black, globose berry, 7-8 mm wide. Coastal hammocks. Florida to Mexico, Central America, and West Indies. All year. (Fig.86)

   2. **Eugenia foetida** Pers. (Spanish Stopper). Tree up to 12 m tall. Leaves 3-6 cm long, obovate, rounded at apex, dark green above, paler beneath. Flowers in axillary racemes with 3 to 6 pairs of flowers; calyx-lobes 4, scarious; petals smooth, 1.5 mm long; stamens about 40. Fruit a globose, dark-red to black berry, 5-7 mm wide. Coastal hammocks. Brevard County southward. Florida to Mexico, Central America, and West Indies. All year. *Eugenia buxifolia* (Sw.) Willd.; *Eugenia myrtoides* Poir.

Fig. 86. *Eugenia axillaris* (White Stopper), × 3/5.

3. **Eugenia rhombea** (Berg) Krug & Urban (Red Stopper). Shrub or small tree to 3 m tall; bark smooth. Leaves 3-6 cm long, ovate, coriaceous, narrowed to a rounded tip, dull green above, paler beneath. Flowers axillary in clusters of 2 to 4; calyx-lobes ciliate, in unequal pairs; petals ciliate, white, 4 mm long. Fruit 7-8 mm wide, black, globose. Hammocks. Lee County southward. Florida to Mexico, Central America, and West Indies. All year.

4. **Eugenia uniflora** L. (Surinam Cherry). Shrub or small tree up to 9 m tall; young stems glabrous or with few reddish hairs. Leaves 3-7 cm long, ovate, bluntly acuminate, base rounded, dark, shiny green above, paler beneath. Flowers in short axillary racemes of 2 or 3 pairs of flowers or solitary; calyx-lobes leaflike, reflexed; petals white, 7-8 mm long; stamens 50 to 60. Berry orange red, very juicy, depressed globose, 2-3 mm wide. Disturbed sites. Brevard County southward. Florida to tropical America. Native of South America. Escaped from cultivation. All year.

2. MELALEUCA

Trees. Leaves alternate, evergreen, coriaceous. Flowers sessile, bracteate, solitary or in dense, elongated spikes, the rachis growing into a leafy shoot after flowering; calyx-lobes 5, deciduous; petals orbicular, spreading, white; stamens many, united into 5 bundles opposite the petals. Fruit a woody capsule with an annular orifice. 100 species. Indomalaysian region and Australia.

1. **Melaleuca quinquenervia** (Cav.) Blake. (Cajeput). Characters of genus. Bark whitish, in soft thick layers, shedding and ragged. Flowers conspicuous, in dense, elongated spikes. Moist soil. Pasco County southward. Native of Australia. Escaped from cultivation. All year. *Melaleuca leucodendron* L. misapplied. (Fig. 87)

Cajeput trees are used as windbreaks or planted as specimen trees. In the southwest counties of Florida they have become a pest, crowding out native species. Eradicating them is almost impossible.

3. MYRCIANTHES (Naked Stopper)

Trees or shrubs. Leaves opposite or ternate. Flowers in cymes, 1- to many-flowered, fragrant; calyx 4- to 5-lobed, persistent; petals 4, white, spreading; stamens many. Fruit a 1- to 2-seeded berry, crowned by the persistent calyx. Ca. 50 species. Florida to tropical America.

1. **Myrcianthes fragrans** (Sw.) McVaugh (Twin Berry). Characters of genus. Leaves simple, aromatic, 2.5-8 cm long, bases wedge shaped, margins entire, revolute. Flowers in long-peduncled cymes of 3 to 14 flowers. Fruit red. Hammocks. Volusia County southward. Florida to tropical America. All year. *Anamonis simpsonii* Small; *Anamonis dicrana* (Berg) Britt.; *Myrcianthes fragrans* var. *simpsonii* (Small) R. W. Long (Fig. 88)

Fig. 87. *Melaleuca quinquenervia* (Cajeput), × 3/5.

Descriptive Flora 159

Fig. 88. *Myrcianthes fragrans* (Twinberry), × 1/2.

4. PSIDIUM (Guava)

Trees or shrubs. Leaves opposite, prominently pinnately veined. Flowers axillary, solitary or in few-flowered cymes; sepals separating irregularly; petals 4 or 5, white, larger than sepals, spreading; stamens many, borne on disk. Fruit a fleshy berry crowned with calyx. 140 species. Tropical America.

1. **Psidium guajava** L. (Guava). Characters of genus. Hammocks and disturbed sites. Pinellas and Brevard counties, southward. Florida, tropical America. Native to tropical America. Escaped from cultivation. All year. (Fig. 89)

Guava is a thicket-forming tree. Fruit is sweet, aromatic, and used for preserves, guava paste, and jellies.

NYSSACEAE (Tupelo Family)

Trees or shrubs. Leaves simple, alternate. Flowers unisexual; staminate numerous, in heads, racemes, or umbels, petals 5 or more, stamens numerous; pistillate solitary, larger than staminate, calyx fused to inferior ovary, petals 5 or more. Fruit dry or drupaceous. 2 genera, 10 species. East Asia and eastern United States.

1. NYSSA (Tupelo)

Trees or shrubs; stems terete. Leaves deciduous, broad, simple, alternate. Flowers dioecious, greenish; staminate flowers 5-parted, petals small; pistillate flowers 5-parted. Fruit a somewhat elongate drupe. 8 species. Eastern United States and Asia.

1. **Nyssa sylvatica** Marsh. (Black Gum). Characters of genus. Leaves 5-15 cm long. Drupe blue black, stone ribbed with shallow grooves. Upland woods, freshwater swamps. Manatee County northward. Florida to Georgia and Delaware. Spring. (Fig. 90)

The trees in central Florida are **Nyssa sylvatica** var. **biflora** (Walt.) Sarg. (Swamp Black Gum). Trunks swollen when growing in water. Leaves narrowly elliptic. Swamp forests. *Nyssa biflora* Walt.; *Nyssa ursina* Small

ARALIACEAE (Ginseng Family)

Trees, shrubs, woody vines, rarely herbs. Leaves alternate, simple or compound. Flowers small, bisexual or unisexual, branched inflorescences; calyx minute; petals 3 to 5; stamens 3 to 5, alternate with petals; ovary inferior. Fruit a berry. 55 genera, 700 species. Tropics.

Fig. 89. *Psidium guajava* (Guava), × 2/3.

Fig. 90. *Nyssa sylvatica* (Black Gum), × 3/5.

1. ARALIA

Trees, shrubs, or herbs, or spiny or smooth. Leaves alternate, pinnately compound. Flowers in compound umbels; calyx minute; petals 5, white or greenish; stamens 5; styles free. Fruit a black berry, tipped with persistent styles. 35 species. North America and Asia.

1. **Aralia spinosa** L. (Devil's Walkingstick). Characters of genus. Stout prickles on stems, branches, petioles. Leaves leathery, 2- to 3-compound, up to 1 m in length. Wet woods. Northern half of our area. Florida to Texas, Delaware, and Missouri. Summer. (Fig. 91)

CORNACEAE (Dogwood Family)

Trees, shrubs, or perennial herbs. Leaves simple. Flowers small, bisexual or unisexual, in heads or panicles; heads may be surrounded by conspicuous petaloid bracts resembling a large flower; calyx tube 4- to 5-lobed, fused to ovary; petals 4 or 5, free; stamens equal in number to petals, alternate with them; disk flattened; ovary inferior. Fruit a drupe or berry. 12 genera, 100 species. Temperate regions.

1. CORNUS (Dogwood)

Trees or shrubs. Leaves opposite (rarely alternate), simple, entire. Inflorescence an umbellate or corymbose cyme or headlike and subtended by 4 involucrate bracts; flowers small, bisexual; 4-merous; ovary inferior. Fruit a drupe, 1-seeded. 4 species. Widely distributed.

1. **Cornus florida** L. (Flowering Dogwood). Characters of genus. Flowers yellow, in dense clusters, surrounded by 4 large, white, petal-like bracts. Fruit scarlet. Hammocks, rich woods. Hillsborough County northward. Florida to Texas, Minnesota, and Maine. Spring. *Cynoxylon floridum* (L.) Raf. (Fig. 92)

ERICACEAE (Heath Family)

Trees, shrubs, or herbs. Leaves usually evergreen, simple, alternate, opposite or whorled. Flowers bisexual (rarely unisexual); solitary or in various inflorescences; calyx 4- to 7-parted, usually persistent; corolla 4- to 7-parted or petals free, funnelform, urn-shaped or campanulate; stamens 8 to 10, often appendaged or terminated by tubules, usually opening by terminal pores or slits; style 1, stigma simple, often lobed. Fruit a capsule, berry, or drupe. 50 genera, 1350 species. Cosmopolitan.

Fig. 91. *Aralia spinosa* (Devil's Walkingstick), × 1/2.

1. Leaves serrate, sessile or with petiole less than 1 cm long; ovary inferior .... 2. *Vaccinium*
1. Leaves entire, with petiole over 1 cm long; ovary superior .... 1. *Lyonia*

1. LYONIA

Small trees or usually shrubs. Leaves evergreen, deciduous, alternate. Flowers white to pink, 5-parted; calyx deeply divided; corolla

Descriptive Flora 165

Fig. 92. *Cornus florida* (Flowering Dogwood), × 1/2.

globose to tubular or ovoid; stamens 10, included, filaments dilated at base; ovary superior. Fruit a globose, 5-ribbed capsule. 30 species. America and Asia.

    1. **Lyonia ferruginea** (Walt.) Nutt. (Rusty Lyonia). Characters of genus. Shrub or occasionally a small, crooked tree to 5 m tall; rusty pubescence. Leaves evergreen, margins rolled inward. Flower globular, angled at base. Moist or dry acid soil. Throughout. Florida to South Carolina. Spring. *Xolisma ferruginea* (Walt.) Heller (Fig. 93)

166 TREES OF CENTRAL FLORIDA

Fig. 93. *Lyonia ferruginea* (Rusty Lyonia), × 1/2.

2. VACCINIUM (Blueberry)

Shrubs or rarely trees. Leaves evergreen or deciduous, alternate, short-petioled, entire or serrulate. Flowers solitary in upper axils or in terminal racemes; calyx 4- to 5-parted; corolla 4- to 5-lobed, tubular, ovoid to campanulate; ovary superior. Fruit a many-seeded berry, crowned by the persistent calyx. About 150 species. Northern Hemisphere.

1. **Vaccinium arboreum** Marsh. (Sparkleberry). Characters of genus. Leaves evergreen, simple, tips rounded, glossy and dark green

above, paler beneath. Flowers fragrant, white, pendent, bell-shaped, constricted at throat. Hammocks, open woods. Lee County northward. Florida to Texas, Missouri, and Virginia. Spring. *Batodendron arboreum* (Marsh.) Nutt. (Fig. 94)

Fig. 94. *Vaccinium arboreum* (Sparkleberry), × 2/3.

THEOPHRASTACEAE (Joewood Family)

Trees or shrubs. Leaves opposite, evergreen, leathery, entire. Flowers bisexual, in racemes, panicles, or corymbs; sepals 5, imbricate; corolla 5-parted, campanulate or salverform; stamens 5, partly fused to corolla tube, staminodes 5; ovary inferior. Fruit a drupelike berry. 5 genera, 110 species. Tropical America and West Indies.

1. JACQUINIA (Joewood)

Trees or shrubs. Leaves evergreen, leathery, numerous. Flowers in erect racemes; calyx persistent; corolla deciduous; staminodes broad. Fruit an erect berry. 50 species. Tropical America.

1. **Jacquinia keyensis** Mez (Joewood). Characters of genus. Twigs crooked, covered with minute gray scales. Leaves yellow green, obovate. Flowers fragrant, yellow, showy. Fruit yellow or orange. Coastal hammocks. Lee County southward. Florida and West Indies. All year. (Fig. 95)

MYRSINACEAE (Myrsine Family)

Trees or shrubs. Leaves alternate, simple, leathery, entire, punctate. Flowers bisexual or unisexual by abortion and dioecious; inflorescence in racemes or panicles; sepals 4 to 6, free or fused; corolla 4- to 6-lobed, rotate or tubular; stamens 4 to 6, epipetalous. Fruit a drupe or berry. 35 genera, 1000 species. Tropics and subtropics.

1. Flowers axillary on short, spurlike peduncles, solitary or in small clusters, on twigs of previous year; fruit less than 5 mm diameter .... 2. *Rapanea*
1. Flowers in terminal panicles or axillary, long-pedunculate cymes; fruit over 5 mm diameter .... 1. *Ardisia*

1. ARDISIA

Trees or shrubs. Leaves entire or serrate. Flowers bisexual or polygamous in panicles, cymes, or clusters; calyx minute, campanulate, sepals deltoid; corolla rotate, tube short, 5-lobed; stamens included, filaments very short. Fruit a drupe, globose, 1-seeded. 400 species. Pantropical.

1. **Ardisia escallonioides** Schlecht. & Cham. (Marlberry). Characters of genus. Hammocks, pinelands. Volusia County southward. Florida to Mexico, West Indies. All year. *Icacorea paniculata* (Nutt). Ludw. (Fig. 96)

Descriptive Flora 169

Fig. 95. *Jacquinia keyensis* (Joewood), × 1/2.

Fig. 96. *Ardisia escallonioides* (Marlberry), × 3/5.

2. RAPANEA (Myrsine)

Trees or shrubs. Leaves entire, often lepidote. Flowers small, unisexual or polygamous in subglobose clusters in leaf axils or above leaf scars; sepals free or fused, dotted with glands; petals partially fused at base, dotted with glands; stamens lack filaments; ovary globose; style short or absent. Fruit dry or berrylike. 200 species. Tropics and subtropics.

1. **Rapanea punctata** (Lam.) Lundell. Characters of genus. Leaves mostly near ends of branchlets. Coastal hammocks. Levy, Volusia counties southward. Florida, American tropics. All year. *Rapanea guianensis* Aubl. [*Myrsine guianensis* (Aubl.) Kuntze] misapplied. (Fig. 97)

SAPOTACEAE (Sapodilla Family)

Trees or shrubs, with milky sap, armed or unarmed. Leaves simple, alternate, entire. Flowers bisexual, small; calyx 4- to 9-parted or sepals free; corolla 4- to 9-parted; stamens 5 to 20, inserted on corolla tube, some staminoidal; ovary superior. Fruit an indehiscent berry. About 50 genera, 800 species. Tropics and subtropics.

1. Plants more or less thorny; leaves oblanceolate, mostly less than 7 cm long .... 1. *Bumelia*
1. Plants not thorny, leaves lance-ovate, mostly over 7 cm long 2
 2. Leaves densely rufous-sericeous beneath .... 2. *Chrysophyllum*
 2. Leaves glabrous 3
3. Young stems and pedicels with brown or rusty colored pubescence; pedicels as long as or longer than petioles .... 3. *Manilkara*
3. Young stems and pedicels glabrous; pedicels shorter than petioles .... 4. *Mastichodendron*

1. BUMELIA (Milk Buckthorn)

Trees or shrubs; branches usually thorny. Leaves alternate or subopposite, somewhat pubescent beneath. Flowers 3 to many in cymes or clusters; calyx 5-lobed; corolla 5-lobed, each lobe with a pair of lateral appendages, white; staminodes petaloid. Fruit a black berry with a large ovoid seed. 60 species. Tropics, subtropics, and temperate regions of America.

1. Leaf blades not conspicuously reticulate, veins not raised 1. *B. celastrina*
1. Leaf blades conspicuously reticulate, veins raised 2
 2. Pubescence on lower surface of leaves rusty-woolly, not lustrous .... 2. *B. lanuginosa*
 2. Pubescence on lower surface rufous-sericeous, lustrous .. 3. *B. tenax*

172 TREES OF CENTRAL FLORIDA

Fig. 97. *Rapanea punctata*, × 7/10.

1. **Bumelia celastrina** HBK (Saffron Plum). Trees or shrubs up to 8 m tall; stems glabrous. Leaves evergreen, fascicled, oblanceolate, 1-4 cm long. Flowers few to several in axillary cymes or umbels; calyx lobes 2 mm long, ovate; corolla 3-4 mm long, lobes irregularly toothed. Fruit a berry, cylindrical, 7-13 mm long. Coastal hammocks. Florida to Texas. All year. *Bumelia angustifolia* Nutt. (Fig. 98)

2. **Bumelia lanuginosa** (Michx.) Pers. (Gum Bumelia). Tree to 6 m, usually a shrub. Leaves evergreen in our area, simple, alternate or clustered, rusty-woolly beneath, 3-8 cm long, elliptic. Flowers in small, crowded clusters on previous year's twigs; calyx lobes suborbicular, 3 mm long; corolla white, 5 mm wide; staminodes ovate, 2 mm long. Fruit a shiny berry, black, ovate, 10-15 mm long. Dry sandy woods. Pinellas County northward. Florida to Texas, Illinois, and Georgia. Summer.

3. **Bumelia tenax** (L.) Willd. (Tough Bumelia). Tree or shrub to 9 m tall; stems silky-pubescent. Leaves evergreen, oblanceolate, 3-7 cm long, densely tomentose beneath. Flowers in axillary cymes; calyx lobes 1-2 mm long, orbicular-ovate; corolla 4-5 mm wide, ovate-orbicular; staminodes 2 mm long, obtuse. Berries obovoid, 12-14 mm long. Coastal dunes and scrub interior. Middle Florida northward. Florida to South Carolina. Spring. *Bumelia megacocca* Small; *Bumelia lacuum* Small

2. CHRYSOPHYLLUM (Satinleaf)

Trees or shrubs. Leaves evergreen, alternate, commonly lustrous-pubescent beneath. Flowers in axillary fascicles or solitary; sepals 5; corolla lobes 5-7, suborbicular, often pubescent; stamens 5-7, epipetalous; staminodes absent. Fruit berrylike. 150 species. Tropics and subtropics.

1. **Chrysophyllum oliviforme** L. (Satinleaf). Characters of genus. Hammocks, pinelands. East coastal counties. Florida and West Indies. All year. (Fig. 99)

In a breeze Satinleaf becomes a mass of shimmering brown as the undersides of the leaves are exposed.

3. MANILKARA (Sapodilla)

Trees. Leaves alternate, leathery, glabrous, clustered at ends of branches. Flowers in axillary fascicles or solitary; bisexual; sepals 6, biseriate, persistent, reflexed in age; corolla lobes 6; stamens 6; staminodes 6, petaloid or nearly obsolete. Fruit a subglobose berry, topped by a persistent style. 70 species. Pantropical.

Fig. 98. *Bumelia celastrina* (Saffron Plum), × 2/5.

Descriptive Flora 175

Fig. 99. *Chrysophyllum oliviforme* (Satinleaf), × 1/2.

176 TREES OF CENTRAL FLORIDA

1. **Manilkara zapota** (L.) v. Royen (Sapodilla). Characters of genus. Hammocks and old fields. Broward County southward. Native of Central America. All year. *Sapota achras* Mill. (Fig. 100)

4. MASTICHODENDRON (Mastic)

Trees or shrubs. Leaves alternate, evergreen, ovate, smooth. Flowers in axillary fascicles; 5-merous. Fruit a yellow, juicy berry. 9 species. Tropical or warm regions of America, Africa, and southeast Asia.

1. **Mastichodendron foetidissimum** (Jacq.) H.J. Lam. (Wild Mastic). Characters of genus. Tree to 25 m tall; trunk massive, columnar; bark exfoliating into platelike scales. Leaves yellow green, glossy,

Fig. 100. *Manilkara zapota* (Sapodilla), × 2/3.

long-petioled. Flowers yellow, in small clusters on leafless portions of the twigs. Coastal hammocks. Volusia County southward. Florida, Bahama Islands, and West Indies. Spring–summer. *Sideroxlyon foetidissimum* Jacq. (Fig. 101)

EBENACEAE (Ebony Family)

Trees or shrubs. Leaves alternate, entire. Flowers bisexual or unisexual; pistillate flowers solitary, calyx deeply lobed into 3 to 7 parts, persistent, enlarging with age; corolla of 3 to 7 petals partially united at base; stamens 2 to 4 times as many as lobes of corolla. Fruit a berry. 3 genera, 500 species. Tropics and subtropics.

1. DIOSPYROS (Persimmon)

Trees or shrubs. Leaves alternate, entire. Flowers unisexual, axillary, cymose, or the pistillate solitary; calyx 3- to 7-lobed; corolla urn-shaped, white or yellow, spreading or recurved lobes; staminate and pistillate flowers of different sizes; stamens 3 to many, in 2 rows, unequal, filaments pubescent. Berry leathery, subglobose. 500 species. Tropics, subtropics, and extending to temperate zone in North America.

1. **Diospyros virginiana** L. (Persimmon). Characters of genus. Tree to 15 m tall; bark deeply checkered. Fruit yellowish brown, smooth, globose, somewhat flattened, 2-4 cm thick, edible when ripe. Woods, fields, and roadsides. Desoto County northward. Florida to Texas, Connecticut, and Iowa. Spring. *Diospyros mosieri* Small (Fig. 102)

SYMPLOCACEAE (Sweetleaf Family)

Trees or shrubs. Leaves alternate, leathery, entire or toothed. Flowers bisexual or polygamo-dioecious, in close or open clusters; sepals 5, partly united; petals 5, partly united; stamens numerous in several series, partly united to corolla tube; ovary superior. Fruit drupaceous or berrylike. 1 genus, 200 species. Mostly South American.

1. SYMPLOCOS (Sweetleaf)

Trees or shrubs. Leaves often evergreen, thick. Flowers densely clustered; calyx usually persistent; corolla deciduous, yellowish; stamens exserted, conspicuous; style columnar. Fruit a drupe, crowned by the calyx. 200 species. South America and temperate United States.

Fig. 101. *Mastichodendron foetidissimum* (Wild Mastic), × 3/5.

Descriptive Flora 179

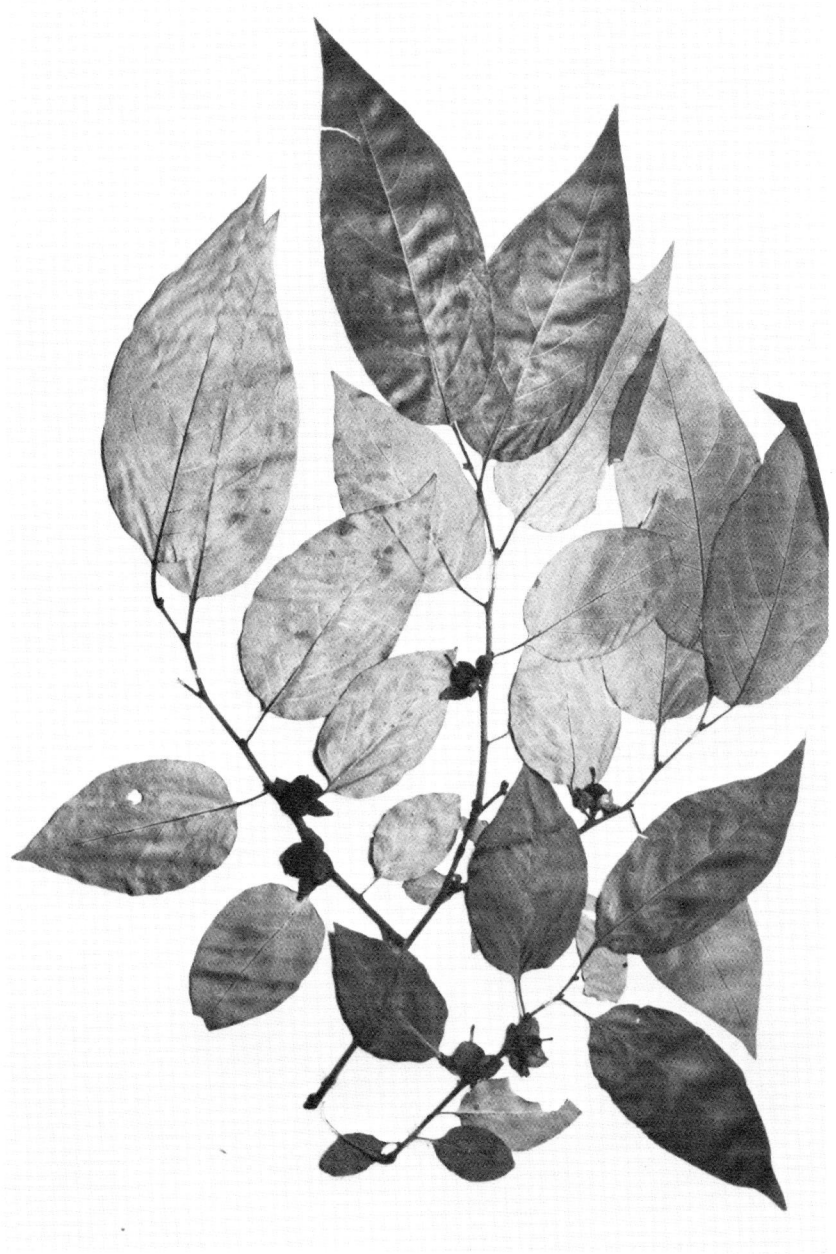

Fig. 102. *Diospyros virginiana* (Persimmon), × 2/5.

1. **Symplocos tinctoria** (L.) L'Her. (Sweetleaf). Characters of genus. Leaves 4-15 cm long, tomentose beneath, yellow green, sweet-tasting. Fruit orange brown. Hammocks and swamp margins. Hillsborough County northward. Florida to Louisiana, Arkansas, and Delaware. Spring. (Fig. 103)

Fig. 103. *Symplocos tinctoria* (Sweetleaf), × 2/5.

OLEACEAE (Olive Family)

Trees, shrubs, or vines. Leaves opposite (rarely alternate), simple, entire or toothed or pinnately compound. Flowers bisexual, calyx with 4 or 5 lobes; petals 4 or 5, free or fused or corolla absent; ovary superior. Fruit a drupe, capsule, or berry. 29 genera, 600 species. Tropical and temperate regions.

1. Leaves pinnately compound; fruit a samara .... 3. *Fraxinus*
1. Leaves simple; fruit a drupe or berry 2
   2. Corolla absent .... 2. *Forestiera*
   2. Corolla present 3
3. Corolla rotate, with elongate, straplike petals;
young inflorescence spreading or drooping .... 1. *Chionanthus*
3. Corolla funnel-shaped, lobes rolled inward;
young inflorescence erect .... 4. *Osmanthus*

1. CHIONANTHUS (Fringetree)

Small trees or shrubs. Leaves opposite, deciduous, simple, entire. Flowers bisexual, in loose panicles from axils of leaves of previous year; calyx deeply 4-lobed; corolla white, lobes narrowly linear, elongate; stamens 2, inserted on corolla tube, anthers large, filaments short. Fruit an oval to subglobose drupe. 2 species. America and Asia.

   1. **Chionanthus virginicus** L. (Fringe tree). Characters of genus. Pistil of fertile flower much larger than that of sterile one; petals 15-30 mm long. Rich woods, along streams. Sarasota County northward. Florida to Texas, Missouri, and New Jersey. Spring. (Fig. 104)

2. FORESTIERA

Trees or shrubs. Leaves simple, opposite, deciduous or rarely evergreen. Flowers dioecious or polygamo-dioecious, small, in lateral fascicles of nearly sessile flowers or in small panicles; calyx minute or none; corolla absent; stamens 2 to 4. Fruit a small, black drupe. 15 species. American tropics and subtropics.

   1. **Forestiera segregata** (Jacq.) Krug & Urban (Florida Privet). Characters of genus. Leaves evergreen, elliptic, entire, 3-6 cm long. Coastal hammocks. Coastal counties. Florida to Georgia and West Indies. Spring. *Forestiera porulosa* (Michx.) Poir. (Fig. 105)

3. FRAXINUS (Ash)

Trees. Leaves opposite, deciduous, pinnately compound. Flowers unisexual (occasionally bisexual), in dense clusters, axillary cymes or panicles from previous year's growth; calyx small, 4-lobed; petals none;

Fig. 104. *Chionanthus virginicus* (Fringe Tree), × 2/5.

Fig. 105. *Forestiera segregata* (Florida Privet), × 2/5.

stamens 2; ovary with 1 style. Fruit a samara. 70 species. North temperate regions.

1. Trees with several trunks; samaras broad, obovate . . . .1. *F. caroliniana*
1. Trees with single trunks; samaras narrow, lanceolate
   to linger .... .2. *F. pennsylvanica*

   1. **Fraxinus caroliniana** Mill. (Pop Ash). Characters of genus. Leaves with 5 to 9 leaflets, 5-10 cm long. Body of samara flat, 4-5 cm long, elliptic, the wing extending to its base. Swamps and cypress heads. Sarasota and Okeechobee counties northward. Florida to Texas, Missouri, and Virginia. Spring. *Fraxinus pauciflora* Nutt. (Fig. 106)

   2. **Fraxinus pennsylvanica** Marsh. (Green Ash). Characters of genus. Tree to 30 m tall. Leaflets 6-12 cm long, entire or undulate; hairy lines along midribs of underside of leaflets. Moist hammocks. Marion County northward. Florida to Alabama, Missouri, and New York. Spring.

4. OSMANTHUS

Small trees or shrubs. Leaves evergreen, simple, opposite, entire. Flowers small, unisexual or bisexual, in axillary or terminal panicles, greenish or white; calyx 4-lobed; corolla 4-lobed, funnel-shaped; stamens 2. Fruit an ovoid or globose drupe, 1-seeded, bitter. 15 species. Subtropics.

1. **Osmanthus americana** (L.) Gray. (Devilwood). Characters of genus. Leaves 5-15 cm long with petioles 1-2 cm long. Swamps, hammocks, Highlands County northward. Florida to Louisiana and Virginia. Spring. *Amarolea americana* (L.) Small (Fig. 107)

A variant of **Osmanthus americana,** in the interior sand scrub area at the southern end of the Lake Region, has much larger, globose fruit and may be referred to as var. **megacarpa** (Small) Green.

BORAGINACEAE (Borage Family)

Trees, shrubs, or herbs. Leaves mainly alternate, simple, entire or shallowly toothed. Flowers bisexual, cymose, often scorpioid; sepals 5, free or partly fused; corolla of 5 partially united petals, tubular or funnelform; stamens 5, alternate with petals; ovary superior. Fruit drupaceous or of 4 nutlets. About 110 genera, 2400 species. Tropics and subtropics.

1. CORDIA (Cordia)

Trees or shrubs. Leaves evergreen, petioled. Flowers terminal in

Fig. 106. *Fraxinus caroliniana* (Pop Ash), × 2/5.

Fig. 107. *Osmanthus americana* (Devilwood), × 1/2.

branched or scorpioid cymes; calyx united to the middle or above; corolla funnelform; style 2-branched above middle, branches 2-parted. Fruit a drupe, partly enclosed in calyx. 250 species. Pantropical.

1. **Cordia sebestena** L. (Geiger Tree). Characters of genus. Shrub or tree to 10 m tall; bark rough, dark brown. Leaves 10-12 cm long, ovate, undulate or shallowly toothed. Flowers 3-4 cm wide, orange corolla lobes. Drupe white, ovoid, 2-3 cm long. Hammocks. Lee County southward. Florida, West Indies, and South America. Summer–fall. *Sebesten sebestena* (L.) Britt. (Fig. 108)

Fig. 108. *Cordia sebestena* (Geiger Tree), × 3/5.

VERBENACEAE (Verbena Family)

Trees, shrubs, or herbs; stems quadrangular or terete. Leaves simple, usually opposite, entire or divided. Flowers bisexual in terminal heads of spikes, or axillary cymes; calyx of 4 or 5 lobes, campanulate or tubular; corolla of 4 or 5 lobes, salverform to rotate; stamens 4 (2 to 5), didynamous; ovary superior. Fruit dry, a berry or drupelike. 75 genera, 3000 species. Tropics and subtropics.

1. CITHAREXYLUM (Fiddlewood)

Trees or shrubs. Leaves opposite, evergreen, shiny. Flowers small, in axillary or terminal spikes or slender racemes; calyx campanulate, obscurely 5-lobed; corolla salverform, limb somewhat oblique, 5-lobed, white; stamens 4 or 5, epipetalous, staminodium present. Fruit a drupe of 2 nutlets. 115 species. Tropical America.

1. **Citharexylum fruticosum** L. (Fiddlewood). Characters of genus. Leaves 5-15 cm long, alternate or subopposite. Flowers fragrant. Fruits shiny, black, juicy, subglobose, 1 cm long. Hammocks and pinelands. Brevard and Manatee counties southward. Florida and West Indies. All year. (Fig. 109)

The very hard, fine-grained wood can be used to manufacture musical instruments, thus the name "fiddlewood."

AVICENNIACEAE (Black Mangrove Family)

Trees or shrubs; roots long, horizontal, producing aerating branches (pneumataphores). Leaves opposite, evergreen, simple, entire. Flowers bisexual, in axillary or terminal cymes or spicate clusters; sepals 5, corolla 4-parted, campanulate-rotate; stamens 4, epipetalous; ovary superior. Fruit a compressed, oblique capsule, pubescent, 1-seeded. 1 genus, 15 species. Maritime tropics.

1. AVICENNIA (Black Mangrove)

Characters of Family

1. **Avicennia germinans** (L.) L. (Black Mangrove). Tree to 20 m tall; bark dark, scaly; young stems pubescent. Leaves shiny above, tomentulose beneath, 3-12 cm long. Coastal shores and swamps. Coastal counties. All year. *Avicennia nitida* Jacq. (Fig. 110)

The complicated root system of black mangrove catches and retains debris, extending the shoreline and preventing erosion. The flowers have abundant nectar, which the bees convert to a clear, white honey with a characteristic flavor.

RUBIACEAE (Madder Family)

Trees, shrubs, or herbs. Leaves opposite or whorled, with interpetiolar or foliaceous stipules. Flowers mostly bisexual; calyx 4- to 5-parted, fused to ovary; corolla 4- to 10-lobed, funnelform or tubular; stamens as many as corolla lobes, alternate with them; ovary inferior. Fruit a capsule, drupe, berry, or nutlet. 500 genera, 6000 species. Widely distributed, chiefly tropical.

Descriptive Flora 189

Fig. 109. *Citharexylum fruticosum* (Fiddlewood), × 1/2.

190 TREES OF CENTRAL FLORIDA

Fig. 110. *Avicennia germinans* (Black Mangrove), × 3/5.

1. Flowers in dense spherical heads .... 2. *Cephalanthus*
1. Flowers in cymose clusters 2
    2. One sepal petaloid; fruit dry .... 3. *Pinckneya*
    2. Sepals not petaloid; fruit pulpy .... 1. *Casasia*

1. CASASIA (Casasia)

Trees or shrubs. Leaves opposite, leathery. Flowers in axillary cymes; sepals 5- or 6-lobed or truncate, campanulate; corolla salverform or almost rotate, 5- or 6-lobed, white or yellow; stamens 5 or 6, filaments adnate to the tube. Fruit a pulpy berry. 10 species. Florida, Mexico, and West Indies.

1. **Casasia clusiifolia** (Jacq.) Urban (Seven-Year Apple). Characters of genus. Leaves clustered at branch tips, obovate, 5-15 cm long. Coastal dunes and hammocks. Broward and Lee counties southward. Florida and West Indies. All year. (Fig. 111)

2. CEPHALANTHUS (Buttonbush)

Small trees or shrubs. Leaves opposite or whorled, deciduous. Flowers densely crowded in spherical heads; calyx 4-parted, short; corolla 4-parted, tubular; stamens 4; style filiform, stigma capitate. Fruit nutlike, obpyramidal. 17 species. Tropics and subtropics.

1. **Cephalanthus occidentalis** L. (Buttonbush). Leaves ovate, lanceolate, or obovate, 5-20 cm long. Flowers 2-3 cm wide, peduncles long; corolla white; flowers arranged between filiform bractlets. Swamps and wet ground. Nearly throughout. Florida to Texas, Minnesota, and Maine. Spring. *Cephalanthus occidentalis* var. *pubescens* Raf. (Fig. 112)

3. PINCKNEYA (Fever tree)

Trees or shrubs. Leaves opposite, simple, entire, deciduous, elliptic or ovate, 5-20 cm long. Flowers in terminal cymose clusters; 5-merous; 1 sepal greatly expanded, petallike, rose pink; corolla 2 cm long, greenish yellow. Fruit a globose to ovoid hairy capsule, 2 cm in diameter. 1 species. Southern United States.

1. **Pinckneya bracteata** (Bartr.) Raf. (Fever tree). Characters of genus. Edges of swamps. Marion County northward. Spring–fall. *Pinckneya pubens* Michx. (Fig. 113)

CAPRIFOLIACEAE (Honeysuckle Family)

Trees, shrubs, vines, or herbs. Leaves opposite, petiolate or sessile,

192 TREES OF CENTRAL FLORIDA

Fig. 111. *Casasia clusiifolia* (Seven-year Apple), × 2/5.

simple or compound, entire or toothed. Flowers bisexual, in axillary or terminal cymes; calyx 5-lobed, fused to ovary; corolla 5-lobed, sometimes 2-lipped; stamens 5, epipetalous; ovary inferior. Fruit a berry, capsule, or drupe. 12 genera, 450 species. North temperate.

1. VIBURNUM (Arrowwood)

Trees or shrubs. Leaves simple, opposite, entire to palmately lobed or toothed. Flowers in terminal or axillary cymes; sepals 5, minute; corolla rotate to campanulate, 5-lobed; stamens 5, epipetalous, ex-

Fig. 112. *Cephalanthus occidentalis* (Buttonbush), × 2/3.

serted; styles 3, sessile at top of ovary. Fruit a 1-seeded drupe. 200 species. Subtropics and temperate regions.

1. Leaves spatulate, short-petiolate or sessile . . . . 2. *V. obovatum*
1. Leaves elliptic to obovate, distinctly petiolate 2
    2. Leaves finely serrate; peduncle less than 5 mm long .3. *V. rufidulum*
    2. Leaves crenate, undulate or entire; peduncle over
       5 mm long . . . . .1. *V. nudum*

Fig. 113. *Pinckneya bracteata* (Fever Tree), × 2/5.

1. **Viburnum nudum** L. (Possum Haw). Small tree or shrub. Leaves thick, long-elliptic, oval or long-obovate, (3-) 5-12 cm long, bases cuneate, apices abruptly acuminate to acute, upper surface lustrous, lower surface rusty-scurfy. Cymes peduncled, 4- or 5-branched, 4-14 cm broad. Drupe globose to elliptical, deep blue with a waxy bloom. Swamps and bayheads. DeSoto County northward. Florida to Texas, Kentucky, and Connecticut. Spring.

2. **Viburnum obovatum** Walt. (Black Haw). Low tree or shrub up to 4 m tall. Leaves 2-6 cm long, oblanceolate, elliptic to obovate, entire

or serrate near apex. Flower small in rounded cymes; corolla white, 4-6 mm wide; stamens short. Drupe ovoid, black, 6-7 mm long. Hammocks and swamp margins. Nearly throughout. Florida to Virginia. Spring. (Fig. 114)

3. **Viburnum rufidulum** Raf. (Rusty Black Haw). Small tree or shrub; bark checkered in small blocks. Leaves sharply serrate, oval, suborbicular to lanceolate, lower surface with rusty red tomentum; petioles often broadly winged, rusty red satiny. Cymes sessile, 3- to 5-branched. Drupe dark blue, glaucous, 10-14 mm long. Upland, well-drained woods. Hernando County northward. Florida to Texas, Kansas, and Virginia. Spring.

ASTERACEAE (Composite Family)

Herbs, shrubs, or rarely trees. Leaves mainly alternate, entire, toothed or divided. Flowers small, bisexual or unisexual, crowded into heads on common receptacles, surrounded by an involucre of 1 to several series of bracts; calyx a pappus of bristles, scales, or awns, or wanting; corolla of several more or less united petals, or wanting; stamens 5, united by their anthers forming a tube around the style, epipetalous; ovary inferior. Fruit an achene, often crowned by the pappus. About 1000 to 2000 genera, 20,000 species. Worldwide.

1. BACCHARIS (Groundsel)

Trees or shrubs; stems much-branched. Leaves alternate, leathery, entire or toothed. Heads dioecious, in panicles of many florets, unisexual; pistillate heads with yellowish green, tubular, filiform florets; staminate florets funnelform; pappus of capillary bristles. Achenes 10-ribbed. About 400 species. Tropics and subtropics.

1. **Baccharis halimifolia** L. (Groundsel Tree). Characters of genus. Tree to 4 m tall, usually a shrub. Leaves 4-6 cm long, coarsely toothed. Heads distinctly peduncled in spreading panicles; involucre strongly imbricate. Achenes with pappus of long white hairs, giving heads a silvery appearance. Hammocks, marshes, and beaches. Throughout Florida to Texas, Massachusetts, Arkansas. Fall. (Fig. 115)

Fig. 114. *Viburnum obovatum* (Black Haw), × 3/5.

Fig. 115. *Baccharis halimifolia* (Groundsel Tree), × 3/5.

Glossary

achene – a dry, 1-seeded indehiscent fruit.
accrescent – increasing in size after flowering.
acuminate – tapering gradually to a pointed apex.
acute – tapering abruptly to a sharp point.
adnate – fusion of unlike structures.
aggregate – crowded into a cluster.
alternate – appearing on one side of the axis and then on the other, as alternate leaves.
ament – a catkin; a slender flexible spike of unisexual flowers, as in the willow.
annular – in the form of a ring.
apetalous – lacking petals.
apex – tip.
appressed – closely pressed against.
arborescent – treelike, becoming a tree.
aril – a fleshy and often colored outer covering of a seed; enlarged ovule stalk.
attenuate – gradually becoming very narrow or slender.
awn – a bristlelike appendage.
axillary – in an axil.
baccate – berrylike, pulpy, fleshy.
berry – a fleshy fruit without a stone usually containing many seeds embedded in the pulp.
bilateral – having two sides which are equal, arranged on two sides.
bipinnate – doubly-pinnate, twice-pinnately compound.
biseriate – in two rows or series.
bisexual – having both sexes on the same plant, having both stamens and pistils in the same flower or inflorescence.
bloom – the white powdery layer on some plants or fruits.
bract – a reduced leaf just below the inflorescence, flower or flower part.
bracteate – having bracts.
bractlet – a secondary bract borne on the pedicel or a secondary branch.
ca. – abbreviation for circa; about.
calyx – the sepals, collectively; the outer set of the floral envelope.
campanulate – bell-shaped calyx or corolla.
capillary – hairlike, very slender, as capillary bristles.
capitate – head or headlike.
capsule – dry, dehiscent fruit.
carpel – one member of a compound pistil; a simple pistil.
catkin – an ament; a bracted spike of unisexual, apetalous flowers.
chartaceous – papery; thin, hard, stiff.
ciliate – bearing fine hairs arranged on the edge of a flattened structure as a leaf, petal or samara.
claw – the long narrow base of some petals or sepals.
coalescent – union by growing together. See also *adnate*.

column – the united style and filaments (as in the Malvaceae).
coma – the tuft of hairs, at the apices or bases of some seeds.
compound – composed of two or more similar and united parts, as a leaf made up of two or more leaflets.
cone – the fruit of coniferous trees consisting of a woody axis on which are arranged stiff, leaflike scales which contain ovules or pollen.
confluent – merging or blending together.
connate – similar structures joined as one body or organ.
contorted – twisted together, bent.
cordate – heart-shaped, with the notch and lobes basal.
corolla – the petals of a flower, collectively; the inner whorl of the perianth.
coriaceous – with leathery texture.
corrugated – wrinkled or minutely furrowed.
corymb – a flat-topped indeterminate inflorescence, the outer flowers opening first.
corymbose – corymblike.
costa – a ridge or midrib of a leaf.
costapalmate – the midrib extends most of the way along the frond, as in *Sabal palmetto*.
crenate – scalloped or shallowly round-toothed on the margin.
cuneate – wedge-shaped; triangular with the narrow end at point of attachment.
cupule – a cup-shaped involucre of many imbricate, closely appressed whorls of bracts, as in the acorn.
cyme – a broad, flat determinate inflorescence, the central flowers opening first.
cymose – like a cyme; bearing cymes.
deciduous – falling after one season's growth; not persistent.
decurrent – the base extending downward on the stem like a wing, as in thistles.
dehisce – to open spontaneously when ripe for the escape of seeds, pollen, etc.
dehiscent – opening or dehiscing when ripe.
deltoid – broadly triangular.
dentate – toothed, the sharp or coarse teeth perpendicular to the margin.
diadelphous – stamens with filaments united into two often unequal groups.
didynamous – with 4 stamens, in two pairs, usually of different lengths.
digitate – having parts or segments originating from a common point, as fingers from a hand.
dioecious – having staminate and pistillate flowers on separate plants.
discoid – having only disk flowers in the head.
disk – enlarged outgrowth of the receptacle.
drupaceous – pertaining to drupes.
drupe – a 1-seeded, usually dehiscent, fleshy fruit with seed enclosed in a stony endocarp.
eglandular – without glands.
ellipsoid – a football-shaped solid.
elliptic – oblong with regularly rounded ends.

emarginate — with a shallow notch at apex.
endemic — occurring in one limited region or area of distribution.
entire — with a continuous, even margin; without teeth, lobes or divisions.
epipetalous — having the stamens seated on the petals or corolla; arising from the petals.
epiphyte — a green plant attached to or depending upon another plant for support but able to manufacture its own food.
excrescences — outgrowths other than spines, thorns, hairs, etc.
exfoliate — to peel off in thin layers.
exserted — projecting out or beyond, as stamens projecting beyond the corolla tube.
exstipulate — without stipules.
falcate — sickle-shaped.
fascicle — a bundle or close cluster.
fasciculate — crowded into bundles or clusters; growing in spiral or whorled fascicles.
filament — thread; the stalk of the stamen, terminated by the anther.
filiferous — filamentous, thread bearing.
filiform — threadlike; long and very slender.
flabellate — fan-shaped, as a palmetto frond.
floret — a small flower, one of a cluster, as in the Asteraceae.
foliaceous — leaflike in texture or appearance.
follicle — a dry fruit, developed from a single ovary, dehiscent along one suture.
foliose — bearing numerous leaves.
funnelform — pertaining to a united corolla limb which is shaped like a funnel.
genus (genera pl.) — the principal subdivision of a family, a closely related group of plants comprised of one or more species.
gibbous — swollen on one side, usually basal.
glabrate — nearly glabrous, or becoming glabrous with age.
glabrous — without hairs or trichomes.
gland — a secreting organ or part.
glaucous — whitened with a bloom.
globose — globular or spherical.
gynophore — stalk of ovary.
heteromorphic — varying from normal structure.
hirsute — with rather rough or coarse hairs.
husk — the outer coating of various seeds and fruits.
hypanthium — the enlarged cuplike receptacle in some plants in which sepals, petals, and stamens are inserted.
imbricate — overlapping.
included — not protruded; opposed to exserted.
indehiscent — not opening spontaneously at maturity, as a fruit.
inferior ovary — embedded into the receptacle below the other floral parts.
inflorescence — the flowering section of a plant.
internode — the part of the axis of a stem between the nodes.
interpetiolar — between the petioles.
intrastaminal — inside or between the whorls of stamens.
involucel — a secondary involucre.

involucrate — having an involucre.
involucre — a whorl or collection of bracts surrounding a flower cluster or a single flower.
keel — the two anterior united petals of a papilionaceous flower; a central dorsal ridge.
labiate — differentiated into an upper and lower portion. Used to describe corolla or calyx of irregular flowers.
lanceolate — lance-shaped, much longer than broad, widest below the middle, tapering to the apex.
legume — a fruit from a single ovary usually dehiscent along two sutures; the fruit of the Fabaceae.
lenticel — raised, corky spots on young branches; a breathing pore in the bark of trees and shrubs.
lepidote — scurfy, with small scales.
limb — the broad portion of a petal; in particular, the expanded part of a corolla with the edges of petals united.
linear — long and narrow, the sides parallel or nearly so.
lip — the principal part of a bilabiate calyx or corolla.
locular — pertains to a seed cavity of a carpel; having one or more locules.
locule — compartment or cavity of an ovary, fruit or anther.
maritime — confined to the seacoast.
membranous — with a thin and usually pliable texture.
-merous — a suffix which when taken with a numerical prefix indicates the number of each of the floral parts.
mesic — an area of average moisture conditions.
monodelphous — stamens with the filaments united into a single tube.
monoecious — with staminate and pistillate flowers on the same plant.
mucronate — terminated abruptly by a short, sharp point.
node — a joint where a leaf is borne.
nut — a hard, dry, indehiscent 1-seeded fruit.
oblanceolate — lance-shaped, but with the widest part above the middle.
oblique — slanting; unequal sided.
obovate — inversely egg-shaped in outline.
obovoid — inversely egg-shaped solid.
obpyramidal — inversely pyramidal, apex at bottom.
obsolete — not evident or apparent; rudimentary.
obtuse — blunt, rounded at the end.
ocrea — sheathing stipules as in the Polygonaceae.
orbicular — circular, round.
orifice — an opening.
ovary — the basal part of the pistil which encloses the ovules.
ovate — egg-shaped in outline, two-dimensional.
ovoid — egg-shaped solid.
palmate — lobed, divided or ribbed in a palmlike or handlike fashion.
panicle — an inflorescence in which the branches of the primary axis are racemose and the flowers pedicillate.
paniculate — resembling a panicle.
papilionaceous — butterflylike, as the corollas of the pea flowers; having a flower with a banner, wings and keel.

pappus – the downy or feathery bristles or scales on an achene representing the calyx lobes in Asteraceae.
pedicel – the stalk of one flower in a cluster.
peduncle – stalk of a flower cluster or a solitary flower.
pellucid – clear or almost transparent.
peltate – supported by a stalk attached near the center of the lower surface, umbrella fashion.
pendulous – hanging downward.
pendent – hanging from its support.
perianth – the calyx and corolla collectively, particularly if they are of the same color.
persistent – remaining attached after the growing period; not deciduous.
petal – one member of the series of flower parts forming the corolla.
petaloid – resembling a petal in color and texture.
petiole – the leaf stalk.
phyllode – a broadened petiole which takes the place of a leaf blade.
pinna – a leaflet or a branch of a pinnately compound leaf.
pinnate – with leaflets or veins on each side of a common stem or vein in a featherlike arrangement.
pistil – the seed-bearing organ of a flower normally consisting of an ovary, style and stigma.
pistillate – with pistils but no functional stamens; female, having pistils only.
plicate – folded, as in a fan; plaited.
pneumatophore – an aerial structure which grows vertically upward from roots embedded in mud, as in black mangrove.
polygamous – having unisexual and bisexual flowers on the same plant.
pome – a fleshy, many-seeded fruit derived from a compound, inferior ovary as in apples and pears.
pseudopapilionaceous – having a flower which resembles that of a pea; falsely papilionaceous.
puberulent – minutely pubescent, the hairs being soft, straight, erect and very short.
pubescent – hairy or downy; commonly the term is used to indicate hairiness of a generalized instead of specialized type.
punctate – with translucent or colored dots, or depressions, or pits.
pyriform – pear-shaped.
raceme – an inflorescence composed of pedicelled flowers arranged along the axis which elongates for an indefinite period. The lower flowers bloom first.
racemose – having racemes.
rachis – the axis of a pinnate leaf or an inflorescence.
radial symmetry – capable of equal division in more than one direction through the center.
receptacle – the more- or less-enlarged end of the flower stalk or the enlarged end of the peduncle which bears the flower of a composite flower.
recurved – bent or curved downward.
reflexed – abruptly bent or turned downward.
reniform – kidney- or bean-shaped.
reticulate – netted or in a pattern which appears like a network.

Glossary   203

revolute — rolled back or up from the margin or apex.
rotate — spreading; wheel-shaped or saucer-shaped.
rufous — reddish brown.
rugose — wrinkled, uneven, rough.
saccate — forming a sac; pouchy.
salverform — descriptive of a corolla composed of a slender tube abruptly expanding into a flat or saucer-shaped top.
samara — a dry, indehiscent fruit with a wing as in ash, elm, or maple.
samaroid — winged like a samara.
scabrous — rough to the touch, with minute rough projections, stiff hairs, scales.
scale — a small, thin bract or leaflike structure, usually dry and appressed.
scarious — dry, thin, membranous, nongreen.
scorpioid — coiled like a scorpion's tail; like a fiddle-neck.
scurfy — with scalelike or flaky particles on the surface.
sepal — one of the separate parts of the calyx.
sericeous — silky.
serrate — saw-toothed along the margin, with the teeth pointing forward.
serrulate — minutely serrate.
sessile — without a stalk.
sheath — a more- or less-tubular structure surrounding an organ or part.
simple — pertaining to a leaf with a single undivided leaf per petiole.
sinus — the bay, recess, or cleft formed by leaf lobes.
spadix — a spike with a fleshy or succulent axis, the flowers often embedded in the axis and subtended with a leaflike spathe.
spathe — the leaflike bract subtending a spadix or flower cluster.
spatulate — spatula- or spoon-shaped, oblong with the basal end long and tapered.
species — a unit of classification composed of individuals that exhibit characters that distinguish the members of this unit from other units within a genus.
spicate — spikelike.
spike — a type of inflorescence in which the flowers are sessile on the sides of a long common peduncle or rachis.
spine — a strong and sharp-pointed woody body mostly arising from the wood of the stem.
spinescent — spiny.
spinulose — with small spines over the surface.
sporophyll — the pollen-bearing part of a flower typically composed of a filament and anther.
staminate — having stamens but not pistils.
staminode — a sterile stamen, usually filament only; sometimes petallike.
staminodium — imperfect organs occupying the position of and resembling stamens.
standard — the broad, erect, upper petal of a papilionaceous flower.
stellate — star-shaped, applied to hairs that are branched.
stigma — the tip of a pistil which is receptive to pollen grains.
stipe — a special stalk under the pistil of a flower, as a stipe of an ovary or legume.

stipitate – borne on a stipe or stalk.
stipule – an appendage, usually green and leaflike at the base of a petiole, usually in pairs.
stipulate – with stipules.
stoloniferous – producing stolons.
stolon – a basal branch rooting at the nodes.
strobilus – an inflorescence marked by imbricated scales or bracts, as in pine cones or *Ostrya*.
style – the tubular upper or middle part of a pistil connecting ovary and stigma.
sub- – a prefix indicating almost or nearly.
suborbicular – nearly circular.
subtend – to be under or opposite to, as a bract beneath a flower.
subulate – awl-shaped; tapering gradually from the base to apex.
succulent – juicy, fleshy and thickened.
superior ovary – an ovary positioned above the calyx.
suture – a line along which dehiscence may occur; a longitudinal seam.
symmetrical – balanced, the parts similar to each other.
terete – cylindrical and tapering, approximately circular in cross section, but of varying diameter.
terminal – at the end point.
ternate – in threes, branching in threes.
terrestial – growing on land.
tomentose – woolly, hairy, densely covered with matted hairs.
tomentulose – with relatively short, fine woolly hairs.
tomentum – wool.
torulose – knobby; with irregular swellings at close intervals.
trichome – a hair or bristle.
truncate – cut off abruptly, blunt as if cut off.
tube – the united portion of a corolla whose petals are fused at least at the base.
tuberculate – warty, having rounded projections or tubercles.
tubercle – a wartlike or knoblike protuberance.
turbinate – top-shaped; more or less as an inverted cone.
turgid – swollen tissue from internal water pressure.
umbel – a flat-topped inflorescence in which the pedicels are of nearly equal length and arise from a common point. A *compound umbel* is an umbel of umbels.
umbellate – in the form of an umbel.
undulate – wavy margin or surface.
unisexual – of one sex; staminate or pistillate only.
urceolate – hollow and shaped like an urn, widest below the open top.
valvate – meeting by the edges but not overlapping; opening by valves.
valve – the area between two lines of dehiscence; one of the segments of an open capsular fruit.
vernation – the arrangement of leaves in a bud.
vexillum – the upper petal in a papilionaceous flower.
whorl – pertaining to a circular arrangement of leaves or flowers on an axis.
wing – a thin, dry membranous or leathery expansion on the surface of an organ, as of a fruit or stem; also the two lateral petals of a papilionaceous flower.

Index

Acacia, 88
  farnesiana, 89, 90
Acacia, Sweet, 89, 90
Acer, 134
  negundo, 134
  negundo ssp.
    latifolium, 134
  rubrum, 134, 135
  rubrum var.
    trilobum, 134
  saccharinum, 134
  saccharum, 135
  saccharum ssp.
    floridanum, 136
ACERACEAE, 132
Aesculus, 136
  pavia, 136, 137
Albizia, 89
  lebbeck, 89, 91
Amarolea, 184
  americana, 184
Amyris, 104
  elemifera, 107
ANACARDIACEAE, 123
Anamonis, 157
  dicrana, 157
  simpsonii, 157
Anise tree, 66
ANISE TREE FAMILY, 66
Annona, 67
  glabra, 68, 70
  squamosa, 68
ANNONACEAE, 67
Apple, Custard, 67
  Pond, 68, 70
  Seven-year, 191, 192
  Sugar, 68
AQUIFOLIACEAE, 129
Aralia, 163
  spinosa, 163, 164
ARALIACEAE, 160
Ardisia, 168
  escallonioides, 168
ARECACEAE, 28
Argenter, 135
  saccharinum, 135
Arrowwood, 192
Ash, 181
  Green, 184
  Pop, 184, 185
  Prickly, 110
  Water, 14

Asimina, 69
  parviflora, 69, 71
ASTERACEAE, 195
Avicennia, 188
  germinans, 188, 190
  nitida, 188
AVICENNIACEAE, 188
Avocado, 73
Baccharis, 195
  halimifolia, 195, 197
BALD CYPRESS FAMILY, 25
Basswood, 142
  Carolina, 145, 146
Batodendron, 167
  arboreum, 167
Bauhinia, 89
  variegata, 89, 93
Bay, Loblolly, 14, 145, 148
  Red, 14, 75, 76
  Swamp, 75
  Sweet, 14, 66
Bayberry, 37
BAYBERRY FAMILY, 35
Bay Cedar, 113, 115
BAY CEDAR FAMILY, 113
Bay Tree, 73
BEECH FAMILY, 42
BEEFWOOD FAMILY, 32
Berry, China, 117, 118
  Soap, 139
  Twin, 157, 159
BETULACEAE, 40
BIRCH FAMILY, 40
BITTERSWEET FAMILY, 132
Blackbead, 101
Black Gum, 14, 160, 162
  Swamp, 162
Black Ironwood, 139, 141
BLACK MANGROVE FAMILY, 188
Blolly, 63, 64
BORAGE FAMILY, 184
BORAGINACEAE, 184
Box Elder, 134
Broussonetia, 51
  papyrifera, 53, 54
Buckeye, 136
  Red, 136, 137

Buckthorn, 141
  Carolina, 142, 143
BUCKTHORN FAMILY, 139
BUCKWHEAT FAMILY, 61
Bumelia, 171
  angustifolia, 173
  celastrina, 173, 174
  lanuginosa, 171, 173
  lacuum, 173
  megacocca, 173
  tenax, 173
Bumelia, Gum, 175
  Tough, 173
Bursera, 113
  simaruba, 113, 116
BURSERACEAE, 113
Buttonbush, 191, 193
Buttonwood, 14, 152, 153
Cajeput, 157, 158
Cajeput Tree, 15, 157
Camphora, 72
  camphora, 72
Camphor Tree, 72, 73
Caper, Jamaica, 78
  Limber, 78, 79
CAPER FAMILY, 75
CAPPARACEAE, 75
Capparis, 78
  cynophallophora, 78
  flexuosa, 78, 79
CAPRIFOLIACEAE, 191
Carica, 149
  papaya, 149, 150
CARICACEAE, 149
Carpinus, 40
  caroliniana, 41
Carya, 38
  aquatica, 38
  floridana, 38
  glabra, 40
  illinoensis, 40
Casasia, 191
  clusiifolia, 191, 192
CASHEW FAMILY, 123
Cassia, 92, 94
  coluteoides, 92, 94
Casuarina, 32
  equisetifolia, 32
  glauca, 33
  litorea, 32, 34
CASUARINACEAE, 32
Cat's claw, 104, 105
Cedar, Atlantic White,

28, 29
  Bay, 113, 115
  Southern Red, 28, 30
CELASTRACEAE, 132
Celtis, 48
  iguanaea, 48
  laevigata, 48, 49
  mississippiensis, 48
  pallida, 48
  smallii, 48
Cephalanthus, 191
  occidentalis, 191, 193
  occidentalis var.
    pubescens, 191
Cercis, 92
  canadensis, 92, 95
Cerothamnus, 38
  caroliniensis, 38
  ceriferus, 38
  pumilus, 38
Chamaecyparis, 28
  thyoides, 28, 29
Chaparral Shrub, 48
Cherry, 83
  Carolina Laurel, 85, 86
  Surinam, 160
  Wild, 85
Chinaberry, 117, 118
Chionanthus, 181
  virginicus, 181, 182
CHRYSOBALANACEAE, 85
Chrysobalanus, 85
  icaco, 86, 87
  icaco var.
    pellocarpus, 86
    interior, 86
Chrysophyllum, 173
  oliviforme, 173, 175
Cinnamomum, 71
  camphora, 72
Citharexylum, 187
  fruticosum, 188, 189
Citron, 108
Citrus, 108
  aurantifolia, 108
  aurantium, 108, 109
  limon, 108
  medica, 108
  paradisi, 108
  reticulata, 108
  sinensis, 108
Coccoloba, 61
  diversifolia, 61
  uvifera, 61, 62

Coccolobis, 61
  laurifolia, 61
Cocoplum, 85, 86, 87
COCO-PLUM FAMILY, 85
COMBRETACEAE, 152
COMBRETUM FAMILY, 152
COMPOSITE FAMILY, 195
Conocarpus, 152
  erecta, 152, 153
  erecta var. *sericea,* 152
Cordia, 184
  sebestena, 186, 187
CORNACEAE, 163
Cornus, 163
  florida, 163, 165
Crataegus, 82
  flava, 82
  floridana, 82
  marshallii, 82, 84
  michauxii, 82
  viridis, 83
CUPRESSACEAE, 27
Custard Apple, 67
CUSTARD APPLE FAMILY, 67
Cynoxylon, 163
  floridum, 163
Cypress, 27
  Bald, 14, 27
  False, 28
  Pond, 26, 27
CYPRESS FAMILY, 27
Cyrilla, 126
  arida, 129
  parviflora, 129
  racemiflora, 126, 129
CYRILLACEAE, 126
Dahoon, 130, 131
Delonix, 92
  regia, 92, 97
Devil's Walkingstick, 163, 164
Devilwood, 184, 186
Diospyros, 177
  mosieri, 177
  virginiana, 177, 179
Dogwood, 163
  Flowering, 163, 165
  Jamaica, 103, 105
DOGWOOD FAMILY, 163

Drypetes, 120
  lateriflora, 120, 121
Earpod Tree, 97, 98
EBENACEAE, 177
EBONY FAMILY, 177
Elaphrium, 117
  simaruba, 117
ELEOCARPACEAE, 142
ELEOCARPUS FAMILY, 142
Elm, 49
  American, 51
  Cedar, 51
  Winged, 51
ELM FAMILY, 47
Enterolobium, 97
  cyclocarpa, 97, 98
ERICACEAE, 163
Eugenia, 155
  axillaris, 155, 156
  buxifolia, 155
  foetida, 155
  myrtoides, 155
  rhombea, 156
  uniflora, 157
EUPHORBIACEAE, 120
Exothea, 136
  paniculata, 138
FABACEAE, 88
FAGACEAE, 42
Fever tree, 191, 194
Ficus, 53
  aurea, 53
  brevifolia, 53
  carica, 53
  citrifolia, 53
Fiddlewood, 187, 188, 189
Fig, 53
  Common, 53
  Shortleaf, 53
  Strangler, 53, 55
Fishfuddle, 101
Flamboyant, 92
Forestiera, 181
  porulosa, 181
  segregata, 181, 183
FOUR O'CLOCK FAMILY, 61
Fraxinus, 181
  caroliniana, 184, 185
  pauciflora, 184
  pennsylvanica, 184
Fringetree, 181
Geiger Tree, 186

GINSENG FAMILY, 160
Gleditsia, 97
  aquatica, 97, 99
Gordonia, 145
  lasianthus, 148
Grapefruit, 108
Graytwig, 59
Groundsel, 195
  tree, 195, 197
Guapira, 63
  discolor, 63, 64
Guava, 160, 161
Guiana Plum, 120, 121
Gum, Black, 14, 160, 162
  Swamp Black, 162
  Sweet, 81
Gumbo Limbo, 113, 116
Gutta-percha, 132, 133
Hackberry, 48, 49
HAMAMELIDACEAE, 78
Hamamelis, 78
  virginiana, 79, 80
Haw, Black, 194, 196
  Green, 83
  Parsley, 82, 84
  Possum, 130, 194
  Rusty Black, 195
  Summer, 82
Hawthorn, 82
HEATH FAMILY, 163
Hercules' Club, 111, 112
Hibiscus, 145
  tiliaceus, 145, 147
Hicoria, 38, 39, 40
  aquatica, 38, 39
  floridana, 39
  glabra, 40
  pecan, 40
Hickory, 38
  Pignut, 40
  Scrub, 38
  Water, 38, 39
HIPPOCASTANACEAE, 136
Holly, 130
  American, 131
  Carolina, 130
HOLLY FAMILY, 129
HONEYSUCKLE FAMILY, 191
Hop tree, 108, 109, 110
Hornbeam, 40

American, 41
Hop, 42, 43
HORSE CHESTNUT FAMILY, 136
Icacorea, 168
  paniculata, 168
Ichthyomethia, 101
  piscipula, 101
Ilex, 130
  ambigua, 130
  cassine, 130, 131
  decidua, 130
  opaca, 131
  vomitoria, 132
ILLICIACEAE, 66
Illicium, 66
  parviflorum, 66, 68
Inkwood, 138
Jacquinia, 168
  keyensis, 168, 169
Jamaica Dogwood, 101, 103
Jatropha, 122
  curcas, 122
Jerusalem thorn, 101, 102
Joewood, 168, 169
JOEWOOD FAMILY, 168
JUGLANDACEAE, 38
Jumbie-bean, 97, 100
Juniper, 28
Juniperus, 28
  silicicola, 28, 30
Key Lime, 110
Krugiodendron, 139
  ferreum, 139, 141
Laguncularia, 152
  racemosa, 152
Lancewood, 73, 74
LAURACEAE, 69
LAUREL FAMILY, 69
Laurocerasus, 85
  caroliniana, 85
Leadwood, 139
Lemon, 108
Leucaena, 97
  glauca, 97
  leucocephala, 97, 100
LINDEN FAMILY, 142
Liquidambar, 81
  styraciflua, 81
Liriodendron, 63
  tulipera, 63, 65
Locust, Honey, 97
  Water, 97, 99

Index   207

Lyonia, 164
 ferruginea, 165, 166
Lyonia, Rusty, 165, 166
Maclura, 56
 pomifera, 56, 57
MADDER FAMILY, 188
Magnolia, 64
 grandiflora, 65
 virginiana, 66, 67
Magnolia, Southern, 65
MAGNOLIA FAMILY, 63
MAGNOLIACEAE, 63
Mahoe, 145, 147
Mahogany, 117, 119
MAHOGANY FAMILY, 117
MALLOW FAMILY, 145
MALVACEAE, 145
Mangifera, 123
 indica, 123, 125
Mango, 123, 125
Mangrove, 149
 Black, 14, 188, 190
 Red, 14, 150, 151
 White, 14, 152
MANGROVE FAMILY, 149
Manilkara, 173
 zapota, 176
Maple, 134
 Silver, 134
 Southern Red, 14, 134, 135
 Southern Sugar, 135
MAPLE FAMILY, 132
Marlberry, 168, 170
Mastic, 176
 Wild, 176, 178
Mastichodendron, 176
 foetidissimum, 176, 178
Mayten, 132
Maytenus, 132
 phyllanthoides, 132, 133
Melaleuca, 157
 quinquenervia, 157, 158
 leucadendra, 157
 leucodendron, 157
Melia, 117
 azedarach, 117, 118

MELIACEAE, 117
Metopium, 123
 toxiferum, 123, 125
Milk Buckthorn, 171
Momisia, 48
 iguanaea, 48
 pallida, 48
MORACEAE, 51
Morus, 56
 alba, 56, 58
 nigra, 56
 rubra, 56
Mulberry, 56
 Paper, 51, 53, 54
 Red, 56
 White, 56, 58
MULBERRY FAMILY, 51
Muntingia, 142
 calabura, 142, 144
Myrcianthes, 157
 fragrans, 157, 159
 fragrans var. *simpsonii*, 157
Myrica, 37
 cerifera, 37
 pusilla, 38
MYRICACEAE, 35
MYRSINACEAE, 168
Myrsine, 171
 guianensis, 171
MYRSINE FAMILY, 168
MYRTACEAE, 152
MYRTLE FAMILY, 152
Nectandra, 73
 coriacea, 73, 74
Negundo, 134
 negundo, 134
Nettle Tree, 49, 50
NYCTAGINACEAE, 61
Nyssa, 164
 biflora, 160
 sylvatica, 160, 162
 sylvatica var. biflora, 160
 ursina, 160
NYSSACEAE, 160
Oak, 42
 Bluejack, 45
 Bluff, 44
 Chapman, 44
 Laurel, 45
 Live, 47
 Myrtle, 45

Post, 47
 Sand Live, 44
 Scrub, 14
 Shumard, 46
 Swamp Chestnut, 45
 Turkey, 45
 Water, 45, 46
OLACACEAE, 56
OLEACEAE, 181
OLIVE FAMILY, 181
Orange, Osage, 56, 57
 Sour, 108
 Sweet, 108
Orchid Tree, 89, 93
Osmanthus, 184
 americana, 184, 186
 americana var. megacarpa, 184
Ostrya, 42
 virginiana, 42, 43
Padus, 85
 virginiana, 85
Palm, Cabbage, 28, 31, 32
 Desert, 32
PALM FAMILY, 28
Papaya, 149, 150
PAPAYA FAMILY, 149
Papyrius, 53
 papyrifera, 53
Paradise Tree, 113, 114
Pariti, 145
 tiliaceum, 145
Pawpaw, 69
 Dwarf, 69, 71
Parkinsonia, 101
 aculeata, 101, 102
PEA FAMILY, 88
Pecan, 40
Pepper Tree
 Brazilian, 14, 15, 128
Persea, 73
 Americana, 73
 borbonia, 75, 76
 borbonia var. *humilis*, 75
 humilis, 75
 palustris, 75
 persea, 73
Persimmon, 177, 179
Physic-nut, 122
Pinckneya, 191
 bracteata, 191, 194
 pubens, 191
Pigeon Plum, 61
PINACEAE, 23

Pine
 Australian, 15, 33, 34
 Longleaf, 14, 25
 Loblolly, 25
 Pond, 25
 Sand, 15, 23, 24, 25
 Slash, 14, 24
 Suckering Australian, 33
Pinus, 23
 australis, 25
 clausa, 23, 24
 elliottii, 24
 elliottii var. densa, 24
 palustris, 25
 serotina, 25
 taeda, 25
Piscidia, 101
 piscipula, 101, 103
Pisonia, 63
 discolor, 63
 discolor var. *longifolia*, 63
Pithecellobium, 101
 guadeloupense, 104
 keyense, 101
 unguis-cati, 104, 105
Plum, 83
 Chickasaw, 83
 Guiana, 120, 123
 Pigeon, 61
 Saffron, 173, 174
 Wild, 83
Poinciana, 92
 regia, 92
Poisonwood, 123, 125
POLYGONACEAE, 61
Pond Apple, 68, 70
Popcorn Tree, 120, 122
Prickly Ash, 110
Privet, Florida, 181, 183
Prunus, 83
 americana, 83
 angustifolia, 85
 caroliniana, 85, 86
 serotina, 85
Psidium, 160
 guajava, 160, 161
Ptelea, 108
 trifoliata, 109, 110
QUASSIA FAMILY, 111
Quercus, 42

austrina, 44
chapmanii, 44
cinera, 45
durandii, 44
geminata, 44
incana, 45
laevis, 45
laurifolia, 45
michauxii, 45
myrtifolia, 45
nigra, 45, 46
obtusa, 45
prinus, 45
shumardii, 46
stellata, 47
stellata var.
  margaretta, 47
virginiana, 47
virginiana var.
  geminata, 45
Rapanea, 171
guianensis, 171
punctata, 171, 172
Redbud, 92, 95
RHAMNACEAE, 139
Rhamnus, 141
caroliniana, 142, 143
Rhizophora, 149
mangle, 149, 150
RHIZOPHORACEAE, 149
Rhus, 125
copallina, 125, 127
leucantha, 126
obtusifolia, 126
vernix, 126
ROSACEAE, 82
ROSE FAMILY, 82
Rose Mallow, 145
Rosemary, 14
Royal Poinciana, 92, 96
RUBIACEAE, 188
RUE FAMILY, 104
Rufacer, 134
carolinianum, 134
rubrum, 134
RUTACEAE, 104
Sabal, 28
palmetto, 28, 31
Sabina, 28
silicicola, 28
Saccharodendron, 135
barbatum, 135
floridanum, 135
Saffron Plum, 173, 174
SALICACEAE, 35

Salix, 35
amphibia, 35
caroliniana, 35, 36
floridana, 35
longipes, 35
marginata, 35
SAPINDACEAE, 136
Sapindus, 138
marginatus, 139, 140
saponaria, 139
Sapium, 120
sebiferum, 120, 122
Sapodilla, 173, 176
SAPODILLA FAMILY, 171
Sapota, 176
achras, 176
SAPOTACEAE, 171
Sassafras, 75, 77
albidum, 75, 77
sassafras, 75
Satinleaf, 173, 175
Saw Palmetto, 14
Schinus, 126
terebinthifolius, 126
Schoepfia, 59
chrysophylloides, 59
Sea Grape, 61, 62
Sebesten, 186
sebestena, 186
Senna, 92
Seven-year Apple, 191, 192
Sideroxylon, 177
foetidissimum, 177
Simarouba, 111
glauca, 113, 114
SIMAROUBACEAE, 111
Soapberry, 139
Florida, 140
SOAPBERRY FAMILY, 136
Sparkleberry, 166, 167
SPURGE FAMILY, 120
Star Anise, 66, 68
Stopper, 155
Naked, 157
Red, 156
Spanish, 155
White, 155, 156
Strawberry Tree, 142, 144
Sugar Apple, 68
Sumac, 124

Poison, 126
Winged, 125, 127
Suriana, 113
maritima, 113, 115
SURIANACEAE, 113
Surinam Cherry, 160
Sweet Gum, 81
Sweetleaf, 177, 180
SWEETLEAF FAMILY, 177
Swietenia, 117
mahagoni, 117, 119
SYMPLOCACEAE, 177
Symplocos, 177
tinctoria, 180
Tallowwood, 60, 61
TALLOWWOOD FAMILY, 56
Tamala, 75
borbonia, 75
humilis, 75
littoralis, 75
pubescens, 75
Tamarind, 104, 106
Tamarindus, 104
indica, 104, 106
Tangerine, 108
TAXODIACEAE, 25
Taxodium, 26
ascendens, 26, 27
distichum, 27
distichum var.
  nutans, 27
TEA FAMILY, 145
THEACEAE, 145
THEOPHRASTACEAE, 168
Tilia, 142
australis, 145
caroliniana, 145, 146
floridana, 145
georgiana, 145
leucocarpa, 145
littoralis, 145
porracea, 145
truncata, 145
TILIACEAE, 142
Titi, 126, 129
TITI FAMILY, 126
Torchwood, 104, 107, 113
Torrubia, 63
bracei, 63
globosa, 63
longifolia, 63

Toxicodendron, 126
vernix, 126
Toxylon, 56
pomiferum, 56
Trema, 48
floridanum, 49
micranthum, 49, 50
Triadica, 120
sebifera, 120
Tulip Tree, 63, 65
Tupelo, 160
TUPELO FAMILY, 160
Twin Berry, 157, 169
Ulmus, 49
alata, 51
americana, 51, 52
crassifolia, 51
floridana, 51
ULMACEAE, 47
Vaccinium, 166
arboreum, 166, 167
Vachellia, 89
farnesiana, 89
VERBENA FAMILY, 189
VERBENACEAE, 187
Viburnum, 192
nudum, 194
obovatum, 194, 196
rufidulum, 195
WALNUT FAMILY, 38
Washingtonia, 32
robusta, 32
Wax myrtle, 37, 38
Whitewood, 59
Wild Lime, 111
Willow, 35
Carolina, 35, 36
Florida, 35
WILLOW FAMILY, 35
Witch-hazel, 78, 79, 80
WITCH-HAZEL FAMILY, 78
Woman's Tongue, 89, 91
Ximenia, 60
americana, 60
Xolisma, 165
ferruginea, 165
Yaupon, 132
Zanthoxylum, 110
clava-herculis, 111, 113
coriaceum, 111
fagara, 111